A PRACTICAL GUIDE TO THERAPEUTIC WORK WITH ASYLUM SEEKERS AND REFUGEES

of related interest

Reading and Expressive Writing with Traumatised Children, Young Refugees and Asylum Seekers
Unpack My Heart with Words
Marion Baraitser
Foreword by Sheila Melzak
ISBN 978 1 84905 384 6
eISBN 978 0 85700 747 6

Writing for Therapy or Personal Development series
Counselling and Psychotherapy with Refugees
Dick Blackwell
ISBN 978 1 84310 316 5
eISBN 978 1 84642 104 4

A PRACTICAL GUIDE TO THERAPEUTIC WORK WITH ASYLUM SEEKERS AND REFUGEES

ANGELINA JALONEN
and PAUL CILIA LA CORTE

Foreword by Jerry Clore

Jessica Kingsley *Publishers*
London and Philadelphia

First published in 2018
by Jessica Kingsley Publishers
73 Collier Street
London N1 9BE, UK
and
400 Market Street, Suite 400
Philadelphia, PA 19106, USA

www.jkp.com

Library of Congress Cataloging in Publication Data
A CIP catalog record for this book is available from the Library of Congress

British Library Cataloguing in Publication Data
A CIP catalogue record for this book is available from the British Library

ISBN 978 1 78592 073 8
eISBN 978 1 78450 334 5

Printed and bound in Great Britain by Bell and Bain Ltd, Glasgow

CONTENTS

PART 1: UNDERSTANDING: THE REFUGEE PHENOMENA

PART 2: THREE CORE PRINCIPLES

PART 3: WORKING WITH GROUPS
AND SEPARATED CHILDREN

PART 4: PRACTITIONERS FIRST AID AND TOOLBOX

FOREWORD

As a solicitor in private practice in London representing asylum seekers and refugees for close to 30 years, I provide advice on immigration, community care and housing to both newly arrived and settled clients, many of whom are highly distressed. While their trauma and distress can often be traced to the persecution they suffered in their home country before fleeing, it is apparent to me that their psychological difficulties and psychosocial needs impact heavily on their capacity to engage with services. As such, my legal work with them is intertwined with their other needs.

To refugees fleeing persecution, the asylum system can seem particularly daunting. While organisations and charities funded to support refugees provide initial signposting services and some guidance, it is to the lawyer that the asylum seeker is directed for professional assistance in navigating the complex asylum process.

It may appear to some that the task of the immigration lawyer is a relatively straightforward one, but coaxing vulnerable and often traumatised clients to tell their story in a clear and persuasive way can be particularly challenging if one lacks a deep insight into their likely mindset and psychological state.

Many clients present with a myriad of issues, from an inability to speak the host language to a fear of the legal process itself. Often, they have been imprisoned or detained before fleeing and will have an inherent distrust of those in authority, with lawyers falling within that bracket. A sensitive approach to client care is essential in such cases, and the client must be put at ease and helped to understand the relevant procedures involved in their case.

If torture is involved, the lawyer must tread a particularly fine line between, on the one hand, eliciting the relevant facts from the client and, on the other, not causing them to become too distressed by reliving their experiences. In addition, cultural differences can add to the complexity and should be borne in mind when trying to arrive at an empathic understanding of the client.

This handbook suggests three core principles to apply when working with refugees: creating a therapeutic relationship to develop trust; bearing witness in order to understand and accurately interpret their experiences; and providing psychoeducation to ensure essential resources to enhance their wellbeing. These three principles provide an effective framework from which professionals can enhance their competence in this client group.

The handbook also explains how to work with interpreters, which can prove invaluable in ensuring that the client is heard and understood.

This book provides an overview of the whole refugee phenomenon, describing the complexity of the refugee experience in a simple and easy-to-read manner. The case studies and learning activities portray the inherent vulnerability yet underlying strengths of refugees, who show such determination to survive adversity.

Over the years I have been practising, I have seen staff burn out in attempting to do their best for our clients. While our work is valuable, it is essential that professionals take time out and also find ways to process distressing narratives in order to remain healthy and objective. This handbook reminds of us the importance of self-care.

I highly recommend this handbook to all professionals who work with asylum seekers and refugees in whatever capacity. It empowers professionals including solicitors, social workers and health services staff by providing them with an overview of the whole refugee experience in a clear and concise way.

Jerry Clore, BA (Hons)
Solicitor Principle of Jerry Clore Solicitors

ACKNOWLEDGEMENTS

This book would simply not have been possible without the immense courage of our refugee clients who have all displayed incredible determination in order to survive and share their individual stories, despite experiencing adversity and danger on long and perilous journeys.

Working with them and bearing witness to their narratives has been a privilege and has informed how we see the world, both in terms of the terrible oppression and abuses of human rights that people endure as well as their capacity to find hope and meaning, which has been profound, powerful and humbling. In doing so, we have learnt so much about ourselves; and for that we cannot thank them enough.

A big thank you to the Refugee Council's Therapeutic Services, where we have a dynamic team that is always keen to learn from our clients in order to inform the work we do and make it better. The team's willingness to regularly review what we do within a changing and volatile environment has contributed to and reshaped our working framework so that it is always fit for purpose. This has kept us motivated to always think about how we should best respond to our clients' disparate needs. The Therapeutic Services team's understanding of the refugee experience within a psychosocial and culturally sensitive perspective — and of the complex issues faced by refugees — has also helped us to think more deeply about how we work safely to avoid secondary trauma, and the need to be compassionate to ourselves when we experience limitations in our practice. The back office staff and volunteers are the backbone of what we do and have also been integral to our value system, setting the foundation on which our practice takes place.

Special thanks to Tony Greenway for his expertise in editing, Sarah Temple-Smith for contributing to the chapter on working with separated asylum seeking children and Dr Lisa Doyle for her feedback which has been invaluable.

Our special thanks go to Senior Management at the Refugee Council for their stewardship and commitment to supporting and empowering refugees to lead safe, dignified and fulfilling lives while they process their asylum claims up to resettlement phase.

We thank the publishers at Jessica Kingsley Publishers for their support and encouragement throughout the writing of this book.

PREFACE

About the Refugee Council

For over 65 years, the Refugee Council in the UK has been one of the leading organisations providing frontline services for asylum seekers and refugees, as well as advocating for their rights.

The organisation delivers key services that respond directly and indirectly to the refugee's needs, through advocacy, casework support, integration, therapeutic services, destitution, resettlement schemes and children services.

Working closely with refugee community organisations and other voluntary and involuntary sectors, their commitment and ethos is to ensure that everyone who seeks asylum is treated fairly and with dignity while they seek safety and start their healing process.

Therapeutic Services is one of the Refugee Council's key services from which the material in this handbook was developed. A dynamic team of psychological therapists provide counselling and therapeutic interventions to asylum seekers and refugees who present with psychological concerns, for the purpose of reducing their distress and enhancing their wellbeing. The team has developed the Therapeutic Care Model based on three core principles (Therapeutic Relationship, Bearing Witness and Psychoeducation) which apply a psychosocial perspective that is sensitive to gender and cultural issues.

This handbook offers a possible insight into the client's world to enhance our empathetic understanding while sharing knowledge, skills and effective interventions that we have learnt while responding to the complex needs of this group.

While this handbook suggests ways in which different disciplines can apply a therapeutic dimension to enhance the efficacy of their work, we also recognise that every client is unique and interventions must take into account their individual and complex needs in order to respond effectively and holistically.

INTRODUCTION

No one leaves home unless home is the mouth of a shark.

Warsan Shire

The world is currently experiencing an unprecedented humanitarian displacement. According to the United Nations (UN), the number of refugees across the globe has reached its highest-ever recorded level, with over 65 million people displaced from their homes as a result of persecution, conflice, violence or human rights violations with many seeking protection in other lands. The UN Refugee Agency puts that startling figure in even starker terms, equating it to 20 people being forced to flee their homes every minute of 2016 (UNHCR 2016). Or, to put it another way, if the total number of the world's refugees formed a nation, it would be the 21st largest nation on the planet (Dearden 2016).

But this book isn't about numbers. Numbers – especially of that alarming magnitude – are both impersonal and overwhelming, and we only quote them here to underline that, but for an accident of birth, the refugee experience could so easily happen to any one of us. That's useful to remember if you are a practitioner or professional working with asylum-seeking or refugee people.

No, this book is, at its heart, about individuals and their personal narratives: people who have fled for their lives to host countries because of invasion, war, tribal conflict, genocide, human rights abuses and political violence, and so on. Once they have reached the safety of another country, that isn't the end of their story, however. For the majority, it's just the beginng. These refugees can face many cultural, environmental, economic and social demands that are completely alien to them. In effect, they have left one potentially deadly situation for a confusing and traumatic one, in a place they do not – and cannot

– comprehend. It is from this context that we have written this book: to help anyone who works with refugees understand their presenting issues, and so respond to them in ways that are effective and appropriate to their needs, while respecting their human rights.

Human rights belong to everyone, regardless of their race, nationality, religion or beliefs. Everyone has the right to life; to have freedom from torture, inhuman or degrading treatment or punishment; the right to liberty and security and the right to a private and family life (Universal Declaration of Human Rights 1948). For refugees, however, most of these have been denied to them in their own lands, and many have been subjected to abuse and violence. They are all escaping from the trauma of danger, imprisonment or death, and have the right to be treated by the authorities in host countries with fairness, equality, dignity and respect.

As frontline staff with the Refugee Council, one of the UK's leading charities, we work directly with asylum seekers and refugees who have fled persecution. This work has been, and continues to be, a great privilege and honour. We are constantly amazed at their resilience and resourcefulness in complex and difficult situations. We can only wonder at their capacity for hope and their unrelenting ability to see possibilities where, at first, there appear to be none. What you'll read over the following pages, therefore, is a collection of our learning over the years about effective ways of supporting and empowering them.

We have divided the book into four sections. The first section is about understanding the context of asylum-seeking and refugee people. The second section focuses on therapeutic ways we have found to be effective in working with this client group. The third section acknowledges the value of community engagement and working with groups and gives an overview of the needs of separated children. The fourth section focuses on what the practitioner needs in order to work safely, and covers best practice when working with an interpreter. We end with our conclusions that consolidate these sections into a unified whole.

We recognise that there is already a wide range of useful resources in this field, so we don't claim that this book is unique; rather we see it as an additional contribution to what is already available. We do, however, hope that it will be useful for caseworkers, solicitors, health professionals, education practitioners and, indeed, anyone working with refugees. If it can be used to inform, support and develop their work in the service of asylum-seeking and refugee people while giving them an ability to achieve their own professional goals and meet their personal needs, then we will have achieved our aim in writing it.

Summary

After reading this book and completing the learning activities provided you should understand:

- the context of refugees' experiences and the impact on their psychosocial wellbeing

- how to apply three core principles to respond to these needs

- how to work with separated asylum-seeking children

- the importance of community involvement in building refugee resilience

- the need for self-reflective practice to enhance service delivery and self-care

- how to work with interpreters

- key learning from our practice.

A note on definitions and terms

To understand the context of asylum-seeking and refugee people, we first need to define key terms.

Who is a refugee?

A person who 'owing to well-founded fear of being persecuted for reasons of race, religion, nationality, membership of a particular social group or political opinion, is outside the country of his nationality and is unable or, owing to such fear, is unwilling to avail himself of the protection of that country; or who, not having a nationality and being outside the country of his former habitual residence as a result of such events, is unable or, owing to such fear, is unwilling to return to it' (UN General Assembly 1951, article 1, A.2).

Who is an asylum seeker?

'A person who has left their country of origin and formally applied for asylum in another country but whose application has not yet been concluded' (Refugee Council 2017).

Disclaimer

We have compiled a collection of three case studies (Mahdi, Priathan and Arufat) to highlight the issues, themes and scenarios that reveal the refugee context and the resulting complexity and dilemmas presented, and which may help to show how best to respond within a holistic framework. The case studies and the names are not real, nor do they represent any particular case; however, the themes are real and reflect collective experiences for learning purposes. Our case studies are from countries with very different attitudes from our own, to illustrate how we might work effectively with these.

Although it is not possible to address every presenting scenario, nor to recommend many other approaches available, we suggest that adapting a curiosity approach that allows learning from the client within a wider psychosocial model is more likely to be effective in responding to their multiple needs. In addition, holding a cultural and gender sensitive approach enables empathic, client-centred, collaborative work for an empowering service delivery.

Refugee background

Apart from refugee children, being a refugee is not a status people are born into but rather one they acquire as a result of circumstances beyond their control. But one may wonder what life was like before their refugee status.

Our three case studies reflect on life before starting the strenuous journey from being a citizen of one country to becoming a refugee in another country and in most cases not of the refugee's choice.

MAHDI

Mahdi came from a country in which the people spoke different languages. However, there was only one official language that was spoken by the dominant and governing tribe, in which all the central government decrees were written. This dominant tribe had superior status to all the others and held the power in the country. Mahdi was privileged as he came from this dominant tribe which assured him of getting good education and opportunities in life.

Mahdi was born into a religious family, as the eldest in a family of five, with one brother and three sisters, he shared the parental responsibilities of caring for his younger siblings. As a young man Madhi was educated and groomed to follow in the footsteps of his father, an elder in the community, which included taking part in family disputes and mediation among community conflicts. It was rare that community disputes or conflicts were taken to court. This was mainly because the courts were marred by injustice and breaches of human rights for the less privileged members of society. The community had formed its own structures of assumed traditional governance, which members adhered to and lived in harmony. His town had a hill on one side and a river flowing along the other. Across the river there was another town belonging to a different ethnic group. The river acted as the symbolic divide to which ethnic group or town one belonged to. The river was important as it was the main water supply for both towns which was also used to irrigate the fields and provide water for their livestock.

As a young boy, Mahdi spent most of his Sundays with his friends learning to swim in the river. He recalled that once when a neighbour's boy drowned in a competition to see who would marry a certain girl in the town. Looking back, Mahdi realised that as all marriages were arranged by parents, this was just a fantasy.

Marriages were mainly conducted to build a bond to strengthen the relationships between the two families. Mahdi recalled how he was excited when his parents found him a potential wife; His motivation to get married was mainly to gain a respectful status in the society in which he could now be trusted with responsibilities, including making decisions. Mahdi first met his wife on the day of their wedding. His wife's family came from a different town but belonged to the same ethnicity which had similar traditions and culture. They were also deemed to be a respected family who held good values. This played an important part in his parent's choice of their son's wife.

Mahdi's father had a large piece of land that he apportioned Mahdi two acres of as a wedding gift. Mahdi reflected that in their tradition, all land and property belonged to the men., and women were protected as part of their household.

Although Mahdi was given these three acres that would remain in his father's name until his death, he was feel to develop it as he wished. Mahdi and his wife got on very well, they fulfilled their roles and responsibilities that were well defined within the community structure. Mahdi worked hard, built a family home on a piece of the land and had four children.

All of Mahdi's sisters had been married off to families who were respected in the community. The third sister had fled her marriage after five years as a result of abuse and violence by her parents-in-law. Mahdi's mother was greatly distressed by her daughter's refusal to conform with family values and blamed herself for the time she allowed her daughter to leave home to study in another city where she suspected she was exposed to other western influences. As a woman, she was expected to submit to her family's will and her protest was deemed to be rebellious and unacceptable both culturally and religiously. Mahdi was fearful that his sister would be ostracised and would be at risk of persecution by the community by being verbally humiliated and social exclusion due to the stigma of her divorced status.

PRIATHAN

Priathan's life before adversity was structured within the desired parameters of her family's expectations. It was important for her to be obedient to her family and sought validation from them in order to gain self-worth. She diligently followed the traditions and family values and although she attended school to secondary level, Her aspirations in life were to be a faithful, committed wife, good mother to her children and a loving daughter-in-law to her husband's parents.

Her role model was her mother who she admired as being the core of the family who kept them united. Throughout her childhood, Priathan helped her mother around the homestead, where she took pride in learning how to cook, clean and decorate the house and also care for everybody else in the family. Doing this helped her to feel safe and self-sufficient. She enjoyed traditional celebrations when she dressed in full cultural attire and was part of a cultural dance troupe who entertained family and guests.

When she became of age, her parents chose her a suitor, according to their culture. They held a religious ceremony in which she was presented with jewellery and other wedding presents. Priathan was happy and looking forward to her new life.

As Priathan did not know her husband before they got married, she was not aware that he was a political activist nor did she consider this her business even when she later found out. She had unconditional love for her husband and trusted that he would look after her in return. It was therefore a shock when her husband left for work one day and did not return. Priathan later realised that she had been preoccupied caring for her mother-in-law and their two daughters that she did not even know where her husband worked. His sudden disappearance and consequent harassment from government agents turned her world upside down.

ARUFAT

Arufat was a qualified doctor in his country and well-known surgeon who specialised in performing caesarean sections. Many women praised his empathic approach and his affordable services. He cared for the less privileged members of society by doing free community work on Fridays after attending prayers in the mosque. Arufat was the sole provider for his family whilst his wife looked after their home and three children. Arufat was a political activist who belived in human rights and a democratic government, he was opposed to the oppressive government regime who supported the president as an individual and the tribe he represented.

He became an informant who passed on sensitive information about government officials who came to the hospital for treatment. As a consequence a bomb was placed in his car which exploded whilst he was driving to work. He was rushed to hospital for treatment where his right leg had been too badly injured to save and had to be amputated. He realised that his activities had been discovered by government agents and that his life was in mortal danger. Furthermore he could no longer provide for his family.

He recalled how vulnerable and helpless he felt and feared for the worst. He could no longer protect his family or himself. He confided in his uncle who helped him find a people smuggler to facilitate him to flee the country and seek safety elsewhere. Once he arrived in a safe country, he rang home and was shocked to learn that one of his daughters had gone missing and there was no system to trace her. His wife's life had also been threatened and she was in a dilemma as to whether she should wait for the return of their daughter, or flee the country for her children's safety. Arufat could not bear to take any more pain as the risk to his family if they stayed was too great , so he urged his wife to take the other children to seek protection in a neighbouring country.

These stories remind us that refugees were ordinary people living normal lives, and that the refugee experience is not a phase in life that is planned but one that is thrust on people when they are caught up in social political situations. Their lives become destabilised and they are forced to seek resettlement in another country. We will now walk into the beginning of this journey of the refugee experience.

PART 1

UNDERSTANDING: THE REFUGEE PHENOMENA

Part 1 of this book is divided into six chapters:

Chapter 1: The Refugee Experience. Understand the four phases of the refugee experience, which we term: Homeland Phase of Apprehension, Persecution Phase of Terror, Asylum Phase of Hope and Fear, and Rebuilding Phase of Relief with Sadness.

Chapter 2: Loss, Separation and Trauma in the Four Phases. Empathise with the impact of loss caused by refugees leaving their home country.

Chapter 3: Host Country Acculturation. Have awareness of both the difficulties and opportunities available in the host country.

Chapter 4: The Complex and Multiple Levels of Needs. Appreciate the many and complex needs these factors create, especially as an asylum seeker who sits between a loss of home and being granted refugee status in the host country.

Chapter 5: Self-Identity and Human Resilience. Have an insight into the impact on one's identity, and be open to ways that asylum seekers respond on a spectrum. This can range from feeling incapacitated to being empowered while facing the challenges the asylum process brings, including integration in the host country.

Chapter 6: Refugee Trauma and Mental Health. The complexities in understanding refugee mental health and how it may differ from your own perspective.

CHAPTER 1

THE REFUGEE EXPERIENCE

You must not lose faith in humanity. Humanity is an ocean; if a few drops of the ocean become dirty, the ocean does not become dirty.

Mahatma Gandhi

The refugee experience is generally described as three stages: 'before, during and after' or 'pre-flight, flight and post-flight' (Hanson and Vogel 2012). Papadopoulos (2002) identifies four, making a distinction in the pre-flight stage between the time before the violence, that he calls 'anticipation', and the actual violence, that he terms 'devastating events'; and names 'flight and post-flight' as 'survival and integration' respectively. We have found this four-phase model to be invaluable in identifying both trauma as well as resilience and strengths throughout each phase of a refugee's journey (Papadopoulos 2007).

Our work with refugees seeking asylum in a host country has been informed by their commonly held emotional responses linked to what is happening at each phase. Namely, apprehension at the prospect of losing their homeland which turns to terror during the actual persecution that forces them to leave. Then hope (of permanent safety) and fear (of a return to persecution) in a temporary sanctuary during the asylum process. Finally, relief when granted refugee status that allows them to rebuild their home in a safe country, yet with sadness as they realise that they may never see their homeland again. We refer to these as: Homeland Phase of Apprehension, Persecution Phase of Terror, Asylum Phase of Hope and Fear, and Rebuilding Phase of Relief with Sadness.

Homeland Phase of Apprehension

Mahdi was a respected elder in the village where he was born and brought up, before war broke out in his country. He was married and they had four children, one son and three daughters. When the war started, Mahdi recalls how they lived in disbelief for five months, constantly listening to the radio in anticipation of the restoration of law and order. Their village supplies of food and electricity were discontinued after four months of fighting, which is when his wife and three daughters fled to a neighbouring country. Mahdi and his son decided to remain behind in order to protect their properties and land.

He said, 'I didn't think the war was going to be serious. I hesitated to make decisions and I did not want to show my family that I was afraid. I did not have enough money to pay for their escape and I could not imagine separating my family. We had always lived together. It was only because of lack of food and electricity that it seemed right that my wife and daughters should go somewhere safe. We could not all afford to leave and I was still reluctant to go. Because of this I didn't say a proper goodbye to my wife and daughters, as I presumed it was just for a short while and they could return to us.'

Mahdi reflected, 'I was also worried about my parents. My youngest sister was looking after them but she is a woman and may not be well equipped to protect them.'

In Priathan's case, she had lived for many months in the apprehension phase. She had first heard about the conflict in her country on the news. When neighbours began to talk about people they knew personally becoming involved, Priathan felt scared; yet she also remembered other times of difficulty that had come and gone, and which she had safely lived through.

Priathan reflected, 'This was the country where I was born, got married and raised my two children. It had never been perfect but we all managed to have a good life. Even when my husband became involved politically, I saw this as positive at the time. I believed that if enough people stood up to protest against the cruelty of the authorities towards its people, they would realise they could not get away with it and stop.'

As a woman, Priathan knew her place when it came to politics. She believed this was a male domain and it would be a disgrace for a woman to share her opinions or have a view on what might be going on, let alone suggest any solutions. She also knew of a woman who was persecuted because she spoke up against the government regime.

'She should have known better. Football and politics belong to men and I have no interest in either,' Priathan added.

Persecution Phase of Terror

Mahdi reflected on his experiences as the war continued in his country.

At this time, Mahdi and a few other community men had identified a safe underground shelter where they took their parents for safety. Although it was crowded and had no windows, at least it would protect them for a while until the country was stable again.

'The government was losing control and the rebels were closing in,' he explained. 'My son was called to help the government fight on the frontline, while I took up the role of hiding and supplying weapons of war to the frontline. Unfortunately, while supplying weapons, I was arrested by the rebels. I was held in a small dark room for five days. The rebels tried to elicit information from me by torturing me. My head was submerged in dirty water and they burned me on my thighs with cigarettes. In the end, I submitted and disclosed sensitive information on a hideout location of senior government officials. After two days, I was being transferred to another location. Fortunately, during transportation, there was a missile attack in which the bus was hit and, in the commotion, I was able to escape.'

'I went back to the site where my son was fighting and discovered that he had been killed in action. Devastated by the death of my son, my betrayal of the government and the impending danger of persecution, I feared for my life and I had no choice but to flee the country through the first available exit route, which gave me no time to find out where my wife and three daughters had fled. I fled and at the same time part of me resisted going, not knowing what lay ahead in the direction I was taking or if it was a safe route to escape. My life was in tatters, I found myself all alone.'

For Priathan, recollecting this phase of persecution was extremely distressing. It was two weeks since her husband disappeared. There were rumours that he had joined the rebels to fight the government-controlling regime to bring change in the country, and this created fear for the family. She had withdrawn her children from school for fear of being harassed along the way.

Soon after this, the government started sending agents to suspected homesteads looking for such rebels or government opponents. Those who were found were arrested for protesting against their regime and such people were tortured or risked a death penalty.

'I could not have imagined they would react with such violence. It was only when I realised that the security forces were prepared to kill me that I made the decision to leave. I had made no plan, and therefore I had no idea of where I was going or how to get there. I was totally unprepared.'

'They tore my clothes,' Priathan stated, looking down and explained what happened when security forces came to her home after her husband was arrested for political activism. She continued, 'They wanted more information about my husband's political involvement, but I did not know any more than I had already told them.' Priathan's shoulders slumped, 'I then realised that, for the sake of my children, I had to leave my country.'

Although Priathan was not a political activist and did not consider herself to be part of the problem, she soon realised that she carried her husband's sins and was equally at risk of persecution for his activities.

This realisation of being in mortal danger, and having to fight, hide, and/or flee marks the second phase: the Persecution Phase of Terror.

Even when living in apprehension for months, or even years, if it becomes clear that to remain will carry the risk of being tortured or killed, people take the actual decision to leave their homeland in an instant. Like Priathan and Mahdi, most people live in denial that they are not safe and partly in hope that things will get better.

Additionally, their country is the place in which they have been raised, developed their self-identity and their status and made other significant attachments. The thought of leaving everything they own behind and walking out into the unknown can be extremely frightening and traumatic. Therefore, when the decision is made to leave, it frequently occurs in haste and *without a plan of where to go and how to get there*, or with sufficient resources to fund the journey.

Asylum Phase of Hope and Fear

The third phase begins when a refugee has to leave their home. Loss of 'home' in this case means many things, including a person's house, country, culture, environment, friends and family.

Priathan reflected on the moment that she reluctantly waved her father and mother-in-law goodbye. She did not shake their hands or hug them, as she was too angry and, at the same time, fearful. She did not want to go and yet she did not have a choice. From an early age, she had been dedicated to caring for her parents and when she got married this included her mother-in-law; however, due to the acts of violence and threat to her life she was no longer able to fulfil this commitment. Such a huge shift in one's purpose in life can be experienced as an overwhelming loss that can impact dramatically on a refugee's self-identity.

Priathan stated, 'I had not discussed with my daughters about what was going on; I could see in their eyes how fearful they were and I was not ready to speak about the danger we were in. I had already paid some smugglers to collect us at night as we did not want our neighbours to know.'

In Mahdi's case the decision to leave his homeland was deeply painful and eroded his self-identity as the protector of his family. He was forced to leave behind all that had made him what he was, his primary role having been to provide for and protect his family. This had now been compromised and he too became a victim of the conflict and war in his country. When crossing through the neighbouring country, he was questioned about his identity by border guards and had to keep his ethnicity secret for fear of further persecution. He stayed in a refugee camp and although water, food, shelter and first aid were available, there was a lack of safety and he witnessed women and children being abused. He felt powerless to protect them, which triggered more fear for his family. This made him more determined to risk crossing the sea into Europe, hoping he would be able to get help to find his family.

Mahdi reflected on his journey, 'I travelled at night and hid during the days along the danger zones. I had to pay and negotiate my way with ruthless and powerful people smugglers. At times, I was vulnerable and had to compromise my dignity for survival. I witnessed various abuses along the way and I helped the weaker ones to keep going. It took me three months before I ended up in Europe without my family and I applied for safety as a refugee.'

This third phase involves a journey, most often to an unknown location by air, land and/or sea. The journey usually involves risk, is often lengthy and, for the whole duration, is outside the protection of any government. This puts refugees at risk of many types of abuse and exploitation.

Priathan was given money by her ailing father for her escape. She felt heartbroken to leave her father behind in such a vulnerable state but he had insisted that she needed to protect her daughters.

Priathan paid an agent and travelled in the back of a truck with her two children.

'It took many, many days. I don't know how many exactly, because we were sealed inside a metal container without any windows. Two men came in with torches every time the truck stopped and brought water and some food for my children.'

Priathan's eyes widened and her voice became hushed, 'They took me to the other side of the container while my children ate.' She appeared frozen and fell silent. 'I prayed silently and constantly. I have always observed our spiritual rituals from my young age but this time I did not feel worthy of God's grace because I felt dirty and had no water to wash myself.'

Priathan had been briefed on the risks of being caught by authorities at various checkpoints, but she was not prepared for what she had to endure throughout the journey, including compromising her dignity by tolerating sexual abuse in order to reach safety.

As Mahdi's and Priathan's stories demonstrate, the journey to escape can be every bit as dangerous and terrifying as the events in their homeland that cause people to flee. Though she had paid them, Priathan experienced the same type of sexual abuse from the people smugglers as she had from the government agents. Indeed, it is frequently the case that smugglers target and exploit refugees before they reach safety and claim asylum in the host country. In Mahdi's case, besides having to deal with people smugglers, he also faced many other physical risks. He endured sleeping rough and walking long distances, and risked his life in an overcrowded boat to cross the sea. When Mahdi claimed asylum, he needed serious medical treatment. He was dehydrated, had an injury from being attacked by an animal while hiding in woodland and had broken his ribs during a storm while on the boat.

On arrival in some host countries, when a person fleeing persecution in their homeland claims asylum, they are given protection under the laws of that land that includes subsistence, food and shelter. However, unless they are granted refugee status, this protection is temporary. If the host country refuses their asylum claim, for example because their case has not been found credible or the country they fled is deemed safe enough, the asylum seeker will be at risk of being removed to their homeland.

Priathan's case, which was made on the grounds of political opinion, was initially refused on the basis that she was not able to demonstrate a 'well-founded fear of being persecuted or being at risk of persecution or "serious harm" and that the state had failed to protect her' (see UN General Assembly 1951, article 1, A.2). Her refusal letter did not reflect her experience or the psychological and physical impact on her but rather reflected more about her husband who had actively opposed the government. As such, she was deemed to be safe in other parts of the country where she could easily relocate.

'I don't understand this process, surely they must know that as a single woman who has been sexually abused, I will be ostracised by my community for having brought dishonour to my family,' she said.

Although Priathan's fear of persecution was clear in her thought process, she had presumed the abuse by her community was common knowledge and had not found it necessary to share such details on her asylum claim. She was extremely fearful to return to her country of origin because she was certain that she would be persecuted. Being in such a dilemma is common, as highlighted in research commissioned by the Refugee Council (McIntyre 2012).

With the support of the practitioner, Priathan was able to connect with her own needs and presented her case more articulately to evidence the fear as directly related to her. She also got a lawyer who listened empathically and understood her from her frame of reference. She made a new statement focused more on her experiences and the breaches to her human rights. Priathan was able to put her case in perspective, noting that on her first application she had focused on her husband's political activities as the base for her claim rather than on her own well-founded fear of being ostracised by the community for bringing dishonour as a result of her sexual abuse by government agents. Her lawyer supported her to make a fresh asylum application under gender-based violence on the grounds of being a member of a particular social group, which is also in line with the 1951 Refugee Convention (Hathaway 1991).

The timeframe for an asylum claim to be concluded varies from case to case, and complex cases can take a long time. Throughout this time, the asylum seeker remains in limbo. They live with the fear of being returned to their home country, potentially to face persecution, as well as the uncertainty of life in a new land. Once they are granted refugee status, the fourth and final phase of the refugee experience begins.

Rebuilding Phase of Relief with Sadness

This rebuilding phase is the point at which an asylum seeker is granted refugee status that provides protection in the host country. While this brings great relief, the label of being a refugee has its own connotations in relation to the social-political attitude and support system in place in the host country. Issues like inequalities in accessing services and limited specialist services to promote refugee mental wellbeing play a significant role in the refugee's ability to integrate.

Now that the fear of being returned to persecution is over, the realisation that they have lost their 'home' also opens a mourning process involving multiple losses.

Mahdi reflected, 'I have lost everything I built with my own hands, such as the family home we lived in. I hold my role as a father and husband in high regard. I had a great traditional wedding where I promised my parents-in-law that I would always care for and protect my family above everything else. However, I have now lost my son in the war and I do not know if I shall ever be reunited with my family in the future. Although I am walking, I feel like an empty shell inside.'

One would imagine that when refugees are granted status in the host country, it would be easier to start rebuilding their life without fear of persecution. However, as Mahdi's case shows, at times this is far from reality. While most of their external and practical needs are met within the support system, the psychological disruption becomes more evident. This is often the case mainly because before being granted refugee status, most refugees are highly anxious and preoccupied with the fear of being returned as they pursue their asylum claim. Once refugee status is granted, they drop the psychological guard that has kept them emotionally stable until that point. This allows their repressed feelings from all they have been through to surface, which, combined with the loss of 'home', is overwhelming as refugees are stripped of multiple elements that define who they are. These include tangible factors such as country, culture, community, friends and family in addition to intangible factors like the weather, harvest time and rituals. All these can cause bereavement and shatter one's identity. Eisenbruch (1990, 1991) termed the loss of things that give meaning to life as cultural bereavement.

LEARNING ACTIVITIES

Think of a time you had a dramatic change in your life, e.g. marriage, new career, new baby, death, divorce.

- What was this experience like?
- What resources did you call upon to cope?
- What did you learn about yourself?

CHAPTER 2

LOSS, SEPARATION AND TRAUMA IN THE FOUR PHASES

You know, those of us who leave our homes in the morning and expect to find them there when we go back, it's hard for us to understand what the experience of a refugee might be like.

Naomi Shihab Nye

As we have seen in Chapter 1, the different phases refugees go through each bring significant challenges involving loss, separation and traumatic events. In the first Homeland Phase it is often impossible to imagine the idea of being separated from one's country, home, family, culture, successful businesses and professional careers, as the case studies illustrate. The persecution often needs to be understood to be as devastating as a nuclear explosion that cannot be survived before the decision to escape (which causes the loss) is finally made. However, for many, once they have left, the desire to return to their home, loved ones, cultural practices and status in society, and to be able to speak to others in their home language, begins. So, if the loss of their homeland is likened to the need to leave an area facing a nuclear explosion, the ongoing separation from their homeland is like the fallout following the blast which continues to poison the place that they would otherwise wish to return to. For the refugee, their homeland remains toxic to them and, furthermore, no matter how terrible the persecution was that caused them to leave, the grounds for refugee status are entirely based on (and require them to demonstrate) this 'persecution in the future' that would await them (Farbey 2002, p.59). Therefore, in the third phase, where safety is not guaranteed by the host country, unless they provide evidence of this future persecution, their fear of being refused asylum can make it hard to mourn the loss of their homeland given that they may still be returned to the danger that poisons it. In the fourth phase, after being granted refugee status, it may be possible to mourn the loss of their homeland yet experience greater separation, such as that from loved ones who still live there.

To help illustrate the differences between these losses and separations we will now explore them in the context of Mahdi's journey through these four phases.

Homeland Phase of Apprehension

'It was like I was in a nightmare. I heard the news on the radio that the neighbouring village had been attacked two months ago but we thought they were robbers. My uncle lost his son when a bomb hit his school; however, I was not willing to accept that we were in danger. I had worked so hard to build my business and provide a good home for my family but I now feared that I would not be able to protect them. This made me very angry towards the government for failing to train the army sufficiently to protect our country.'

In this first phase, prior to persecution, while the loss had yet to happen, Mahdi began to appreciate what he had and did not wish to be separated from.

Mahdi owned land and property and could not simply let go of his life's work and savings. He felt he had failed in his duty as a husband to guarantee protection to his family and so avoided talking about the possibility of leaving everything behind and escaping from danger. Because he did not share these fears with his wife, Mahdi felt increasingly anxious and found it harder and harder to sleep.

When his wife and daughters decided to leave, Mahdi was heartbroken; it was the first time he would be separated from his wife since they got married. He wanted her to stay but realised that he could not guarantee her safety. He was fearful of losing them but letting them go felt as if he was still in control of making the decision to keep his family safe. It was painful to watch his wife sell her wedding jewellery in order to raise enough money to pay their way across the neighbouring country.

The level of his fear and uncertainty caused by the continuing violence was matched by the degree of hope that he would be able to keep what he had, believing that things would get better. He lived in a state of apprehension and denial.

Persecution Phase of Terror

When the news broke that the rebels had attacked and taken control of a nearby village, Mahdi and his son decided to join the government forces to protect the country from the rebels.

Mahdi's wife and children had already escaped to a neighbouring country but his parents had refused to leave, stating that they were too old and that their life belonged here no matter the danger. While Mahdi respected their decision to remain, he was not prepared to leave them in their house which was at risk of being destroyed by the rebels, so he took them to a secret underground shelter for their protection.

Like many of his countrymen, Mahdi lived in hope that if they all fought together against the rebels, they would defeat them and their country would be safe again. However, after a month of fierce fighting, Mahdi was captured by the rebels, 'I was taken to a place called "the cemetery" and was terrified. I thought that my time was up.' Recalling this, Mahdi spoke softly, as if he was back in that place, fearing that the volume of his voice would draw attention and endanger him. 'In that moment, I saw the faces of my children. I began to shake because I believed I would not see them again.'

Such experiences of persecution bring the possibility of death, the biggest personal loss. For some, as for Mahdi, it is not the loss of their own life that is their greatest fear but the loss of loved ones, especially those too vulnerable or young to fend for themselves. Mahdi experienced trauma on many levels in relationship with his own body, with others and with himself. He could not control his hands from shaking and felt shame – less of a man – when he saw others who seemed impassive to the brutality he witnessed. He could not believe how the guards could torture and kill without remorse and doubted if he could ever trust another human being again. Mahdi began to lose his faith in humanity but held on to his faith in God, who he had believed to be a loving and merciful presence ever since he was a young boy.

Mahdi drew a deep breath and continued, 'I could not believe my son had gone for good. If only I had allowed him to stay with his mother, but my pride that we as men need to be strong took control and I encouraged him to defend our country. I did not see him as a child at the time. I am so angry. How can I ever forgive myself?'

Mahdi recalled the day his wife gave birth to his son; there were celebrations in the community for three days. They received many gifts and on the third day Mahdi's father came for the naming and blessing ceremony where his son was anointed to carry the family's name and heritage.

'A part of me died when I lost my son. He carried my family name which would have continued living after my death, I am now afraid that the legacy of our family line might be over if I do not have another son to give it my name.' Mahdi was remorseful and felt helpless.

In the midst of the devastation of losing his son, Mahdi also realised he would be separated from his parents. He was desperate to a have a chance to say goodbye to them but could find no safe route to reach their underground hideout without risking his own life. He yearned to wake and find life back to normal, as the overwhelming sense of loss and separation was too great to bear.

In addition to the fear of losing his loved ones, Mahdi was impacted by the loss of a young boy as greatly, if not more, than if it had been one of his own family. It occurred when he was trekking by night to get to the coast. In the early hours one morning he came across a young boy about eight years old who had also fled, after his parents were killed. He had been left behind by another group who had told him that it was too dangerous to take him with them, but he did not know in what direction he needed to go. Mahdi remembered his son who had died in the war, and he took it upon himself to rescue this boy and take him in the boat with him. About ten miles from the coast they encountered rebel security forces who had set up regular patrols to stop people from escaping. They went into hiding for about four days and became increasingly hungry. Mahdi was haunted by the way the boy looked at him, with desperation in his eyes. Mahdi decided to go alone first, to find a safe route, and then return to pick up the boy. He told the boy to wait there hiding in the bushes until his return. Mahdi went and studied the security pattern and it took him two days to work out when they changed their shifts so that they could pass. Mahdi went back to pick up the young boy but found that he was no longer there. He searched for him in vain. He waited for three days before he accepted that he had to give up. Although Mahdi had

survived torture and managed to escape against all the odds, it was the
yearning expression he saw in the face of the boy that he internalised.
For not rescuing the boy, Mahdi experienced a loss of his self-identity
as a resourceful and strong man who protected children.

'God gave me another chance to rescue a boy and look after him
like my own and I failed again. Why did I leave him behind? He had
all his hope on me and I let him down. I will always remember his
face.'

Mahdi realised that he had not even asked the boy his name.
Although this encounter with the boy was shortlived, the meaning it
had was significant, making it another huge loss for Mahdi.

Asylum Phase of Hope and Fear

The third phase is where the loss of home, the one unique factor that
unites all refugee people (Papadopoulos 2002), becomes apparent.

The journey to exile is one of living in limbo, neither being here
nor there. Along the journey, often through many countries, there is no
safety or protection because they are not recognised by those countries
they pass through. The overwhelming loss of family and friends left
behind is vivid at each moment of the journey.

Priathan found it hard to believe that she had been separated
from her loved ones whom she had left behind; it was like a horrible
dream she wanted to wake up from. She was in denial of the reality
which caused her to feel confused and fatigued, and she often found
herself gazing absent-mindedly into space most of the time: 'As I sat
in the truck while my daughters were asleep beside me, I thought
of all I had lost. Yet, I could not mourn or dwell on my loss as that
was overshadowed by my loss of safety, which left me vulnerable
and fearful.'

'I am looking forward to being with my sister-in-law; this will
give me back part of the family I have lost.' Priathan convinced herself
that living with her sister-in-law would recreate the ideal family she
had lost. This is a common bargaining stage with loss of loved ones,
and a desperate attempt to reclaim life as it had been in the past before
the adversity.

'I remember hearing the start of the engine and seeing the stretch
of water gradually increasing between the coast and the side of the

boat. I began to think about seeing my children…' Mahdi paused. His voice cracked with emotion, 'I didn't say goodbye to my mother.'

Mahdi's story represents that of countless others who escaped war 'with only the shirt on their back'. In the panic to survive, saying goodbye to loved ones frequently does not happen. It is possible that loved ones who are unable or unwilling to leave their homeland will not survive, particularly in a war zone, and it is certain that there will be many experiences of separation. As well as being unable to see those left behind, refugees find that poor lines of communication and loss of contact may result in not even knowing whether relatives and friends are dead or alive.

'I couldn't phone my mother for months because her town was besieged. I saw it being bombed on TV everyday, and lived in constant terror, recognising places I used to go to in ruins, worrying if the underground shelter my mother was in had been attacked and if she was still alive. When I did get through and I heard her voice, I was so relieved.' Mahdi's face lit up when he narrated this, as if hearing his mother's voice had given him a new meaning to life. He then looked sad again, 'My mother said she was not well.'

So, as well as living with the loss of their home, refugees find that loss continues during the journey to safety and also in the host country – they may see people killed while travelling through dangerous environments, such as war zones, turbulent seas and/or desolate regions, or experience the loss of their freedom by people such as traffickers and kidnappers. Even when refugees have reached safety in the host country, complex asylum processes can be traumatic in themselves, involving difficulties accessing accommodation, money and education. Living in poorly maintained housing may also connect them to past loss, that is symbolic of the destruction of their own home. However, it is in the final phase, when safety is granted in the host country, that the loss can be, and frequently is, the most profound of all.

Rebuilding Phase of Relief and Sadness

'I have been granted refugee status!' Mahdi held up the letter from the Immigration Office with the confirmation, and after almost five years of being refused and appealing, his relief was palpable. Then Mahdi looked down, his face became ashen and tears welled up in his eyes as he whispered almost inaudibly, 'I may never see my home again.'

Mahdi experienced what commonly happens once asylum seekers get refugee status. With the relief comes the realisation that they may never go back to their homeland. It may be likened to when a parent dies. This is often when the full impact of the sadness is felt and the grieving process begins.

What makes it more complex for a refugee, however, is that their motherland, unlike a parent who kept them safe and protected, sought to persecute and even kill them. Therefore, the fear of returning to danger and possible death outweighs the sadness they also feel. When they are guaranteed safety by the host country, their new foster parent, this is the time when we witness many refugees connecting with this sadness and breaking down to mourn the loss of the relationship they had with their homeland.

'I haven't seen my mother for over five years and, unless she comes here, I may never see her again.' As well as not seeing his mother, it was also five years since Mahdi lost his son and was separated from his wife and three daughters. Through an international tracing service, he had located his wife and two daughters (one daughter had gone missing during their journey to exile). The sense of loss was huge and his feelings of despair and grief for his son and missing daughter were overwhelming. Mahdi found it difficult to engage with services to start rebuilding his life.

Being unable to do anything except wait for news can create a tremendous feeling of helplessness. In addition, survivor guilt is a common phenomenon experienced by asylum seekers, especially when they are granted refugee status, because they feel they could have done more to save others. In cultures such as Mahdi's, this is further heightened by the obligation to look after one's parents when they are ill or old and to bury them if they die. The psychological distress of not being able to fulfil these duties can be considerable.

'I dreaded how I would cope if my mother died. The friends from my homeland who I met here became extremely depressed when their parents died and they could not lay them to rest. I remember feeling bad about them even though I knew it was not their fault and that I could be in the same position myself.'

Mahdi sounded angry. 'I don't expect you to understand,' he said, and then his tone softened, imbued with a sense of sadness, 'In this country, you seem to be more independent from your parents and I can see there are services to support them.'

This illustrates a key dimension in working with refugees. As we will now consider in the next chapter, while there may be common concerns in which it is possible for an empathic response to be received and shared, cultural differences may make the loss and separation feel that much greater if we are unable to understand their frame of reference. This becomes a very significant issue for refugees in the host country if they feel expected to integrate into cultural practices that are very different from theirs.

LEARNING ACTIVITIES

Using a genogram (see appendix), map out your family tree highlighting those who are alive, dead or living far away.

- What are the dynamics in your family?

- What do you miss about the family who are not present with you?

CHAPTER 3

HOST COUNTRY ACCULTURATION

At the birth of a new world, there will be always pain.

Alex London

After reading this chapter and completing the learning activities provided, you should be able to:

- understand the dilemmas and internal conflicts, as well as the new opportunities that come from living in a different culture

- empathise with ambivalent feelings that asylum seekers and refugees might have for the host country, and realise the impact of this transition as not one of choice but necessity

- understand how a different environment can be disorientating due to tangible factors

- understand the cultural, interpersonal and social factors that influence ability to integrate.

'Acculturation refers to the process of change experienced by immigrants when they come into contact with the members and culture of the host country' (Padilla and Perez 2003, p.35).

The subject of acculturation is a complex one as it has many facets (Berry 1997). The process of acculturation depends on many personal, cultural and experiential factors. During the process, refugees have opportunities to learn new things often previously unavailable in their homeland. At the same time, they may face seemingly impenetrable barriers of communication due to cultural differences with members of the host country and if they speak a different language.

When you have been abroad to a country with a different language and/or cultural norms, what do you experience?

Refugees may experience a psychological 'tug of war' between their homeland culture and adapting to the host country. Factors that influence acculturation include service access, psychosocial activities and the refugee's mental capacity to engage (Berry 1997). Furthermore, the host community needs to be willing to embrace increased diversity and facilitate services access. Specialist programmes designed to respond to the refugee's multifaceted needs and promote refugee integration enhance the acculturation process. However, some host country policies and inequality in services make the process stressful and detrimental to the refugee's psychological wellbeing. This might lead to challenges as well as opportunities.

Women who were not allowed to work can now find fulfilling careers, and men who did not have the chance to bond with their children are now able to participate in their children's care. One big difference in adapting to life in the host culture will be whether an asylum seeker is granted refugee status and awarded equal status in the host country, or remains an asylum seeker who will have to return if their asylum claim is refused. In terms of the four phases, the asylum seeker granted refugee status moves fully into the fourth, rebuilding phase, whereby refugee status is like being given land on which you can build your own home – in this case the land is the country as a whole. For an asylum seeker the third, asylum phase, is lived in great uncertainty, in limbo between the possibility of this fourth phase and the terror of a return to persecution in the second phase. For this reason, while we will identify aspects that will be common to both, we will also explore the differences between what it is like for Mahdi, who has been granted refugee status, and Priathan who awaits a decision of her asylum claim.

After he was granted refugee status, Mahdi was eligible to find employment and work as an equal citizen. However, he experienced overwhelming feelings of bereavement due to his many losses, he lacked motivation and felt ambivalent towards a country with different cultural norms that he didn't choose. He acknowledged that the host country was safe, and that the system provided him with opportunities to develop himself both professionally and personally. However, he also faced dilemmas in the process of adapting to a different culture, language and cultural practices which, when he engaged with them, felt like a betrayal of his own culture.

Mahdi tapped the table and appeared extremely frustrated, 'I knew I could do the job effectively, but because I wasn't able to speak the language fluently my colleagues seemed very impatient when we worked together. I noticed they appeared relaxed when interacting with other members of the team. I neither felt heard nor could I say what I wanted to, and I think this stopped me progressing in the role. My confidence dropped and even though I had a good university degree and experience working in finance, I did not feel I could engage on the same level as my colleagues.'

Mahdi's experience and qualification in finance enabled him to get a job as an accounts clerk; however, his ongoing internal conflicts, psychological distress and lack of fluency in the host country language were barriers to his personal development and reduced his ability to integrate. He was unable to hold a position in his chosen career and got a job as a factory labourer where there was no pressure to speak the language. However, Mahdi was determined to work through the barriers to reach his potential.

'I cannot complain about the challenges I am facing to become part of society. I understand this will take time. I have enrolled in a free language class and found a good charity where they provided conversational group work. I have also started attending part-time volunteer work in a finance department as an accountant. This will give me the skills and experience I need to work in my field of expertise.'

When faced with the difficult process of adaptation, refugees can react by participating in the process or by avoiding it. Mahdi participated in the process of adaptation, accepting that it would take time, patience and understanding to appreciate the cultural differences so that he could feel accepted enough to rebuild his life. The one area he continued to struggle in was in his religious life. Due to his faith as a Muslim, traditionally he dedicated his Friday to a day of fasting and prayer; however, in the host country he was expected to work throughout the weekdays and that included Fridays.

'Friday is the worst day of my week. We used to attend a local mosque where my wife and I were active members and I was a respected elder. I dedicated this day to supporting our community in various ways, including visiting the sick and feeding the poor, which gave purpose and meaning to my life. I now wake up on Friday and block out the significance of this day. I now just go to work and let the day pass by. My life feels empty.'

At a cognitive level, Mahdi recognised the importance of adapting to make the most of opportunities in the host country. Although he initially found it hard to stay present on Fridays, he supressed his cultural needs and was able to cope with this new way of living which facilitated the integration process.

As mentioned in the Introduction, before adversity Arufat had a job as a doctor. He had taken his own inner journey within the new context of his new life. He reflected on the anger and bitterness he had carried due to the overwhelming loss for which he harboured regrets. However, after attending therapy and participating in group meditation, he had started to appreciate his existence and saw that there was still goodness in humanity, as shown through the host country's attitude. He especially valued the emphasis placed on being autonomous and self-actualising. At first, he considered the community as unfriendly and strange because he did not know his neighbours. This would never have been the case back in his own country where the whole community knew each other by names, apart from the small children. He had always seen himself in relation to his family and part of his community. He now realised how he might have been missing out on embracing himself.

'It is like I have just discovered myself after I have lost everything.' Arufat started appreciating himself and saw that he was being recognised in his own right, and that although he had no right to work as a doctor he had something to offer to others who had gone through similar experiences. This experience had changed his philosophy in life. Whereas in the past, personal status, professional success and helping the poor from a privileged position were more important, he now valued humankind, autonomy, humility and the importance of relationships on an equal level.

In Priathan's case, she felt so alienated from her familiar surroundings and overwhelmed by the struggle to integrate that this meant she avoided making contact with local community members.

'I was afraid of leaving my sister-in-law's house. All the streets and houses seemed to look alike and I felt disoriented, not knowing what direction to take. I was also scared to ask for directions from strangers and I stayed indoors unless my sister-in-law accompanied me, even to the local shops.'

Without refugee status, Priathan found it hard to integrate. As an asylum seeker, she remained in a state of limbo between a past full of sadness from loss and a future that held great fear, knowing that if her asylum claim was refused she would most likely be returned to danger. This past and future tug of war was further compounded by a present of uncertainty in a new country where she needed to integrate socially, with regard to different customs and practices and, just as importantly, legally, by abiding by its laws (Papadopolous 2001).

Priathan looked shocked when she reflected on how different it was to raise children here. 'My sister-in-law said social services would take away my children if I continued to use physical discipline when they were naughty.' Priathan became tearful, 'Without my husband it has been so difficult. I never had to discipline the children before, but now he's not here I have to.' Priathan began to sob, 'I know it's hard for my children, but if I don't make them behave, my husband's sister has threatened to kick us out of their home. But how can I if I am not able to smack them? My mother always beat me for my own good and I think it worked for me. This made me anxious, because I knew I needed to find another way to discipline my children. I remain concerned about this, but now I do feel good that I am in a country where everyone, including children, are protected.'

As well as being protected by the law of the land, asylum seekers like Priathan also receive health care and access to the basic needs of housing, food, clothes and subsistence from the host country.

'When my sister-in-law said I would have to leave, I was really scared I would become homeless. However, I am becoming more reassured that in this country we are all protected physically and I am also legally entitled to accommodation with my children if we do become homeless. I've already been to the doctor and had medical tests at the hospital, so I feel more hopeful that my health will improve. The most challenging thing has been that I don't speak the language and no one understands mine, so I am worried that I won't be able to explain what I need.'

The difficulty of not being able to communicate in the language of the host country can be a problem if interpreters are not available, for example for daily tasks like shopping. In addition, this difficulty in communication takes on an even greater significance in regards to their asylum case where it is of the highest importance to have an accurate translation of their claim, to substantiate whether it satisfies the criteria for refugee status.

For Priathan, the process of acculturation was especially difficult because she felt emotionally overwhelmed by her feelings of loneliness due to her isolation, being alone when her two children were at school, and separated from the friends and family in her homeland. These feelings were interwoven with an internal sense of not belonging, accompanied by external criticism in the news where migrants were described as being a drain on public resources. As a consequence, while her two children seemed to integrate well in their school, Priathan felt increasingly isolated and adopted an attitude of avoidance to cope with complex situations. She would give reasons why she was not able to attend her children's parents' evenings or go to cross-cultural events. As a result, she struggled to develop relationships with local community members and also felt obliged to protect her own cultural norms (Phillimore 2011).

The combination of internal issues, such as psychological trauma and perceived alienation in the host country, and external factors, such as not speaking the language and prejudice in the community, play a significant role in the refugee's ability to integrate in the local community.

Another important factor, illustrated by the case studies, is that asylum seekers and refugees face so many changes, and experience such pressure to adapt quickly, it is essential that they receive appropriate assistance to help them navigate the host country system to to help them meet their needs in a timely manner.

In the next chapter, we will explore the ways Priathan met the many needs she had. We will sit in a session with her solicitor, discussing her asylum case. We will have an appointment with her doctor, who attended to the injuries she sustained on her journey; and a meeting with a housing officer, where she found out what she was entitled to with her children.

LEARNING ACTIVITIES

Imagine what it would be like to relocate to a country that was very different to your own.

- Reflect on what aspects of their culture would be different to your own culture.

- What would it be like for you to adjust to that culture?

CHAPTER 4

THE COMPLEX AND MULTIPLE LEVELS OF NEEDS

One of the basic needs of every human being is the need to be loved, to have our wishes and feelings taken seriously, to be validated as people who matter.

Harold S. Kushner

After reading this chapter and completing the learning activities provided you should be able to:

- understand the key services needed to address refugees' psychosocial needs, including practical and basic needs, medical support, legal representation for their asylum case and psychological services that support and empower their wellbeing

- appreciate the inequality in access to services that comes from not speaking the host country's language, and from having different cultural attitudes and laws

- appreciate the different discourses that the refugee interacts with, including legal, medical, advisory and psychological, to meet their multiple needs

- understand how all key services need to work together using a multidisciplinary approach.

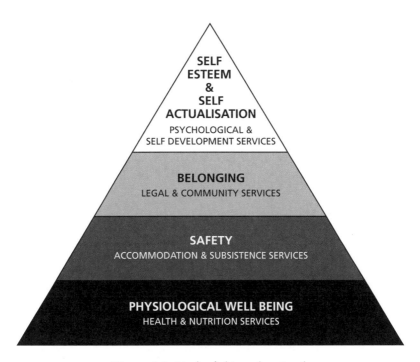

Figure 4.1: Maslow's hierarchy triangle

In this chapter, we will explore how Priathan met her practical needs for physical health and safety by accessing housing and claiming asylum in the host country. We will consider her psychological needs in depth when she accessed counselling in Chapter 6. However, given the impact of loss and separation and host country acculturation, this psychological dimension is vital to factor in at all times, to ensure that a refugee has the capacity to connect to, and so meet, their practical needs. As we will see, this was very difficult for Priathan to do. She struggled to tell her doctor what she needed physically due to being emotionally overwhelmed by shame due to her experience of sexual abuse. She also was unable to assert her need for suitable housing because she had embodied her country's cultural conditioning that women had to behave demurely.

Priathan represents the needs most asylum seekers have. We have found Maslow's hierarchy of needs an essential tool to help assign these into levels of importance.

This hierarchy operates like levels of a pyramid, each providing a foundation from the ground up on which the next is built. The most important priority, the foundation of the pyramid, is given to biological health that first addresses any life-threatening illness or injury and issues caused by factors such as malnutrition and limited immunisation. Having access to food and water is part of this. The second level is current safety, provided by accommodation that gives physical protection. The third is belonging which is attained temporarily when asylum is claimed in the host country, and permanently if their claim is accepted and refugee status is granted.

In Priathan's case, her need for the first level of physical health required medical interventions for the many injuries she and her children had sustained during the journey to the host country.

'My children were suffering from malnourishment. When the war started, we had a very poor diet, virtually no health services operated and only limited immunisation provided by an international organisation. By the time we arrived in the host country, my daughter was suffering from an undiagnosed disease.'

Asylum seekers and refugees are among some of the most vulnerable groups in the world, particularly when it comes to accessing health services. The complexity of their health needs prior to arriving in the host country can be vast. This is mostly due to a lack of health services in their country of origin, experiences of malnourishment, living in environments with poor sanitation, undiagnosed chronic diseases, limited access to immunisations, health deterioration due to imprisonment, torture and sexual assault, psychological trauma and grief and many other issues. In addition, they can encounter similar issues in the countries they travel through en route to the host country. Even if they are in countries that do offer health services, most asylum seekers will be avoiding making contact for fear of being stopped and sent back, so they remain hidden until reaching a country where they can claim asylum.

However, as we have seen with Priathan, on arrival in the host country, these health problems can be exacerbated due to language barriers, a lack of social support, isolation, insufficient knowledge about their entitlements to health services in the host country, and a fear of institutions. In addition, they may be denied services they are entitled to by practitioners who may not have the specialist knowledge required to understand the refugee context.

Then, on the second level of Maslow's hierarchy, immediate physical safety is provided by accommodation and essential needs which create a secure base refugees can feel safe temporarily while they process their asylum claims. Refugee status confers the third level need – belonging – when the host country accepts an asylum seeker as a refugee with equal rights who is then able to integrate fully in the local communities.

To follow Maslow's priorities of need we will begin with Priathan seeing Jane, her doctor, then meeting John, the housing officer, and finally, Laura, her solicitor. Each had booked an interpreter to allow Priathan to communicate her needs.

Priathan saw Jane in her surgery a week after she arrived.

She presented with persistent headaches and had bruises on her legs and arms to which her doctor prescrived painkillers and an antiseptic cream for her bruises.

At the time of seeing the doctor, Priathan had not started to process the traumatic events she had been through, and to cope she developed a psychological defence called dissociative amnesia. This prevented her from connecting to the memory of what had happened because she struggled to acknowledge or accept how she really felt about her traumatic experiences. Priathan knew that she needed medical help but was so concerned that she would re-traumatise herself if she talked about what really happened that she made up a story that would make enough sense of her injuries to the doctor. Although her story was not the truth, it was a narrative that kept Priathan emotionally safe and enabled her to get the treatment she needed for her persistent headaches in the form of medicine that Jane prescribed for her. However, as Priathan did not explain that she had been sexually abused, Jane was unable to offer early intervention that would have significantly accelerated her physical healing process.

At the following appointment, Priathan was seen by a different doctor who was male and as she entered his surgery Priathan left the door open. When the doctor asked her to close the door behind her, this immediately evoked fear within her. The doctor had presumed that she did not understand and spoke with greater volume to make his request clear, at which point Priathan froze. The doctor then got up and closed the door himself. While the doctor had done this to ensure Priathan's privacy, to her this scenario was symbolic and triggered feelings related to a traumatic past experience in which she had been abused within an enclosed space. As a consequence, Priathan became extremely distressed and was unable to explain her medical needs to him.

This account demonstrates the importance of being sensitive to the needs of clients from a refugee background, of providing a safe environment within which relevant information can be brought to light. For example, observing the way pain is somatised in the body may help to identify sexual injury without needing the narrative of the event of actual abuse.

The second basic need of safety was addressed when Priathan met John, the housing officer, a few days after her sister-in-law had said she would soon have to leave.

'When I arrived in the host country I was relieved that my husband's sister came to meet us and gave us a room in her house; however, since this time, the environment has become very hostile. Maybe she is upset because I left her mother behind. I avoid getting close to her because I am afraid she will find out about the abuse that happened to me; it has been getting more and more difficult to cope.' Priathan looked down. She had never lived on her own before and she perceived this option as stigmatising. She was in a dilemma and sat feeling helpless and disempowered. John listened sensitively and explained, 'As an asylum seeker, you may be entitled to your own accommodation.'

This helped Priathan to appreciate that in the host country it was acceptable for women to live alone and be independent. This felt very strange and fearful to Priathan, but it also brought a sense of freedom that she had never experienced before.

Three weeks after the meeting, Priathan and her children were housed in a two-bedroom flat. Unfortunately, the flat had some maintenance issues: the shower did not work properly, one wall had damp and the kitchen light constantly flickered. In the past, Priathan had relied on her husband to deal with such issues, so when she went back to talk to John about this she found it hard to ask for what she needed.

'I need to ask him to send someone to make these repairs urgently but I am afraid that he will think I am demanding and a bad person, especially because I am a single mother.'

John listened to Priathan sensitively and explained that as an asylum sekker with children she was entitled to her own accomodation and that he was happy to support her in applying for this if it suited her.

Priathan held a belief that a wife must behave in a certain way and presented herself as 'nice', not demanding or as prioritising her needs above others. Although Priathan was distressed about the issues with her accommodation, she also carried a lot of shame, which made it difficult to assert her needs or make a complaint about not receiving the service.

She responded in a submissive manner, briefly mentioning the issues but without requesting what she really needed, which we have found to be a common response asylum seekers have with issues in their host country.

In the next meeting with Laura, the solicitor, Priathan faced her biggest challenge. Although she knew that she needed to disclose the terrible things that had happened to her to get refugee status, the distress it caused her when she revisited these events was overwhelming.

Priathan held her documents tightly and spoke nervously, 'It was when security forces came to my home after my husband was arrested for political activism that I realised that, for my children's sake, I had to leave.'

Laura gave Priathan space to talk, enabling her to tell and, when necessary, re-tell her story in a way that made sense both chronologically, as a series of events that were coherent, and psychologically, due to the emotional impact they had.

Because it is common for such narratives to be disjointed and disrupted, due to the distress of reliving the external acts of violence, a holistic approach that encompasses the specified criteria that need to be satisfied to be eligible for a service or treatment, and the individual's response, is required for refugees' needs to be met.

A psychosocial approach

In each of the meetings above, Priathan received a specific service. Each of the professionals was specialised in giving an expert assessment that addressed a vital need. The role of the doctor was to ensure physical health, the housing officer to provide safe housing, and the solicitor to advocate for their protection by the host country. However, due to the refugee context involving trauma and cultural differences, Priathan was not able to express her needs and the professionals were not equipped in ways to support her to identify and meet them.

Given this complexity, we have found that a psychosocial perspective that focuses on intra-psychic, interpersonal and socio-political dimensions is essential in meeting our refugee clients' needs (Papadopoulos 2011). In applying this approach, it becomes possible to see the whole situation and make appropriate interventions if there is a block, as there was for Priathan in accessing her medical needs. In this example, socio-politically, as an asylum seeker in the host country, Priathan had the right to medical treatment. However, in her meeting with Jane, Priathan was intra-psychically overwhelmed by trauma. This impeded their interpersonal communication as it prevented Priathan from disclosing the sexual abuse to Jane and from accessing the support that Jane would have provided her with.

In this example, interventions need to be made to reduce Priathan's intra-psychic distress sufficiently to enable her to communicate her sexual abuse. These interventions could come from one or all of these dimensions. In the intra-psychic dimension, an intervention providing Priathan with therapy, and exercises to psychologically ground herself, could have enabled her to disclose the abuse. This disclosure could also have been facilitated in the interpersonal dimension, if Jane had used a particular type of discourse to elicit the issue of abuse. In the socio-political dimension, disclosure could have come from a policy for medical staff to receive training in working with trauma and in identifying issues such as sexual abuse in refugee populations. From this example, we suggest that such an intervention in the socio-political dimension would provide the most effective way not only for Priathan to have received the medical care she needed but also for all refugees to access treatment from medical services – particularly given that such a policy could provide best practice interventions in the interpersonal and intra-psychic dimensions as well.

Even if we are unable to effect a change at this socio-political level, we hope this example demonstrates the value of keeping this dimension in mind when considering a refugee's multiple levels of needs. We find that Pearce's (1994) framework of multiple layers of context, which shows how each layer can impact the others, is also valuable in this regard. He argues that this level of political context carries the most weight, due to how it oppresses the levels below, therefore placing it right at the top. We have observed in our work with asylum-seeking people without refugee status that, whatever other needs they have, this socio-political level of persecution in their homeland involving their asylum case is constantly impacting the other dimensions. They report it as a cause of great fear at the intra-psychic level and interpersonal level, with many stating that they cannot talk to anyone from their country in case they inform the authorities back home about them. For this reason, we have found that an empathetic understanding of where they are in this socio-political dimension of their asylum case is a prerequisite to the efficacy of the work that we do in the intra-psychic and interpersonal levels. Again, this affirms the value of Maslow's hierarchy of needs and the importance of ensuring that the basic needs of safety are being met.

Style and substance

As this handbook focuses on working directly with a refugee in the interpersonal dimension, we will offer what we have found to be effective for our clients in the way we communicate – the discourse that is used, for example, when disclosing sensitive material. This involves keeping in mind both the substance (the subject involving the material need) and the style (the lens through which this is seen and the discourse by which it is communicated).

The substance is the criteria by which the client's need is evaluated. Medically, this is ascertained through the presentation of physical symptoms, and legally, by assessing the relevance of the client's persecution in relation to the categories that will substantiate their need for asylum, namely: political difference, religion, race, nationality or group.

The style by which these are discussed and described also needs to be understood. For example, the medical and legal professions use a positivistic discourse with an epistemology that seeks knowledge of objective universal truth that requires observable evidence. On this basis, refugee status is granted if the asylum seeker's evidence of persecution in their homeland is ascertained to be fact, and is refused if judged false.

However, as Priathan's experiences show, disclosing facts can pose difficulties for asylum seekers both culturally and psychologically. Culturally it may be inappropriate to speak about certain subjects, for example due to religious reasons or because they are believed to be topics of conversation suitable for expression only by one gender. Psychologically, as we have described, it can be hard for refugees to face the truth of acts done to them or that they themselves did (even if they were necessary for their very survival), due to the shame that they experience. In Priathan's case had her doctor asked her directly for precise information about her sexual abuse it would be likely that she would not have been able to process the question. This is because, even though receiving treatment for the medical condition that this had caused was vital to her health (potentially even saving her life), Priathan became too psychologically overwhelmed by shame to answer.

For these reasons, it is essential to understand both the external reality – the criteria that are required to meet a need – and the internal experience of the refugee.

While it may be necessary to use a positivistic discourse to find out salient information, the manner in which the inner experience of the individual is attended is, we suggest, best served by a phenomenological approach that attempts to 'see the world as it appears to the client', putting aside one's own assumptions and preconceptions (Barker, Vossler and Langdridge 2010, p.125).

In Part 2 of this handbook, we explain how we work to achieve such understanding in detail and hope this will provide ideas for how to apply a therapeutic dimension in your own work with refugee clients.

Before doing so, we look in the next chapter at the impact of the four phases of refugee experience on the self-identity, which Maslow delineates as the higher psychological needs of self-esteem and self-actualisation. We will then conclude Part 1 with a chapter on refugee mental health to assess which interventions are most likely to reduce distress and enhance wellbeing in refugee populations.

LEARNING ACTIVITIES
One of your friends is overwhelmed with life issues which include being out of work, having a mortgage, a difficult relationship and struggling with low moods.

• What plan of action would you take to support him ?

• What immediate interventions might be useful to stabilise him?

• What resources do you need in order to be effective in supporting him?

CHAPTER 5

SELF-IDENTITY AND HUMAN RESILIENCE

I am not what happened to me, I am what I chose to become.

Carl Gustav Jung

After reading this chapter and completing the learning activities provided you should be able to:

- understand how self-identity is shaped by past experiences and the current psychosocial environment

- understand the dilemmas faced by refugees as they negotiate and make sense of their self-identity in order to make informed choices

- understand different levels of impact on identity in relation to the refugee experience.

Having established the basic needs of food, shelter and belonging, we look at Maslow's (1943) higher levels of need – self-esteem and self-actualisation – which both inform self-identity.

While self-identity is formed from birth and influenced by the various developmental stages (Erikson 1968), for refugees there is another dimension to this. They may experience disruption in their lives that can dramatically change their perceived self-identity. This means refugees constantly have to re-evaluate themselves in the light of these new experiences caused by external factors that can impact their internal belief system.

Homeland Phase of Apprehension

Before her homeland went into turmoil, Priathan's life was well defined and she was content with it. She had grown into being a respectable woman who always observed her religious and traditional values; she had earned her parents' pride, which was important to her sense of self-worth.

'I have never lived by myself. As a female, this is not acceptable in our culture. When my parents decided that I was of age, they arranged for my marriage to a man of their choice. I trusted them fully because they loved me and would ensure that I get married to another respectable family. After a ceremony of blessings, I moved from my parents' home to live with my husband and my mother-in-law. My father-in-law had died and it was my duty to look after my mother-in-law as well as my husband and our children. I felt very lucky with the way my life had turned out.'

Priathan's self-concept was based on a collective identity (Melucci 1996), and her beliefs and attitudes were driven by those of her family. Her life was fully intertwined with the members of the family and they responded as a whole, whether in celebrations or in grief. Her loyalty to her parents, husband and in-laws was unconditional and the choices that she made were driven by her family's expectations of her. Having her own needs was deemed secondary to those of her family's needs. In some cases, this could be perceived as selfish and would risk family rejection and alienation. Priathan took her role as a wife, mother and daughter-in-law very seriously and with due diligence in making both families proud.

Persecution Phase of Terror

Priathan's self-concept was thrown into disarray by the actual persecution. The close-knit family unit that operated as her protective factor was no longer available. Priathan's husband had disappeared, her mother-in-law was unwell and her parents could not ensure her safety after they became aware their daughter had been sexually abused. To protect their family honour they encouraged her to flee the country, which went against Priathan's inherent family commitment. Her values, self-worth and belief were all put to the test and she struggled to make sense of this new world in which she found herself. This forced change in her social relations and in her role, which had a significant impact on her identity. Where she previously perceived herself as a self-sufficient, content wife, she now felt exposed, vulnerable and feared that she lacked internal resources to make choices or take appropriate actions.

Conflict and violence shift the social environment and impact people's identity formation on many levels (Bion 1961). As Priathan did not previously have a voice or autonomy, it was very difficult for her to make decisions. Her internal world was shattered when she was first sexually abused by government agents. Her core value to remain pure and loyal only to her husband had been defiled, leaving her highly distressed. She felt betrayed by her family, who she believed would always be there to protect her, and she no longer trusted the world.

Asylum Phase of Hope and Fear

The journey to seek refuge in a safe country can be complex and although it has many risks it also offers a sense of hope, which can be a motivating factor for many asylum seekers. However, this journey can take months, navigating through many dangers to reach safety. Some people travel through borders to nearby refugee camps while others might not make it due to various issues, such as poor health.

For Priathan, while she clung on to hope, she endured many abusive encounters throughout the journey when negotiating the transport arrangements for her and her daughters with the people smugglers. She endured these traumatic experiences in silence and her mind disconnected from what her body was experiencing as a defence, in order to survive: 'I had no choice, my life is no longer important. All that matters now is my children's safety. It is like I do not exist because I do not feel anything inside me.'

Priathan's self-esteem was very low because of her experiences; she found it hard to respect herself and believed others would not respect her either. Her decision to live with her sister-in-law was not based on choice but was more to do with cultural expectation and a strong emotional drive to recreate an extended family similar to the one she had in her home country. Her sister-in-law also lived in an area with high numbers of people from her community whose ways of living were familiar to her, and Priathan found it easier to practise her traditions. For example, the smell of food using spices that she was familiar with stimulated her sense of belonging in this community.

This cultural familiarity reinforced her previous identity, which gave her a sense of belonging and self-regularisation.

However, attending community events had its own drawbacks, as seeing other families with both parents, which she related to as the 'norm', brought back painful memories of her own loss and separation from her husband. Priathan was also deeply saddened by leaving her mother-in-law behind and felt incomplete. She struggled emotionally to accept the decision to leave, even though she knew this was necessary in order to save her children. This is termed as survival guilt (Van der Veer 1992). In addition to the pull of loved ones in her homeland and in the host country, Priathan felt confused about where she stood. It was as if she had a foot in each place, with neither feeling safe. Eisenbruch (1990) referred to this as 'cultural bereavement'.

There are many levels on which identity and self-concept are affected by this process of forced dislocation. Being aware of the different levels is essential in having a holistic perspective of the client in order to support them more effectively. Applying Pearce's framework (1994) enables to to discern which level of context was dominant at a time for the client, while also being aware of the other layers.

On a socio-political level, Priathan's sense of belonging was influenced by her present environment and her past life experiences. She identified herself with all migrants, regardless of their context: 'My sister-in-law has been telling me about the negative information on social media towards immigrants. This makes me feel lonely and I fear going out in case people notice me. I rely on my sister-in-law to accompany me if I need to go somewhere or buy something.'

Priathan reflected on how she now had to rely on asylum support in order to meet her basic needs, 'While I had rights to live in my country as a citizen, I have now become an asylum seeker in a foreign country with limited rights and am dependent on others to support me.' In her country, she was proud to rely on her husband to provide materially while she cared for and raised the family. However, now that she relies on the state, she believes she is a burden and feels uncomfortable going to sign on in order to receive humanitarian support to meet her basic needs.

'My fingerprints were taken and I was given an identity card with a number. I present this card to every office I go as identification.' Priathan felt her identity of being a mother, a daughter, a wife and daughter-in-law had been stripped off and replaced by an identity card with a number. Her 'identity stripping' was compounded and marred by past traumatic experiences of abuse by government agents in her home country and the lack of any protection during the journey to safety from people who would endanger her, such as traffickers and people smugglers. These experiences shaped her identity, which in turn changed her perception of herself and the world.

Having lost her home and become an asylum seeker, Priathan had defined her parameters of 'not belonging' to justify the introjections she was getting from negative social media messages. Although there were also positive messages about migrants, she believed she was not fully accepted, which had an impact on her ability to fully participate as a citizen, and she did not feel safe enough to identify with either nationality.

In the case of Mahdi, although the physical level was most prominent for him at this time, being aware of other levels, like the spiritual level, which for him was key once identified and brought in, played a significant part in containing his distress and facing his hardship.

As an asylum seeker, Mahdi had been preoccupied with uncertainty and fear for his future, but on receiving refugee status, he experienced an emotional dilemma about what this new identity meant to him. He had always seen himself as a patriot of his country, even to the extent of being prepared to die for it.

'Watching my country go into ruins was killing me slowly. I feel helpless and that I have failed my country. However, the fight to regain independence must continue. I have been meeting with people from my country who share and feel this loss and we have decided to start an organisation to have demonstrations and raise awareness to recreate the political ideology that we have lost in my country.' Although Mahdi was not initially a political activist, the experience of losing his country redefined his purpose in life as he developed a strong conviction to do all he could to reclaim his homeland. Papadopoulos (2007) terms this 'adversity activated development'.

As a staunch believer, Mahdi had always lived his life in accordance with his faith. He believed there was one almighty God above everything else, which reassured him he was never alone on this journey and was an anchor to his life. He attributed all positive outcomes, including the reason he had survived, to his belief. Despite the adversity he suffered, Mahdi had never questioned his faith. He also trusted in God that he would be able to see his family again. With deep humility, Mahdi had accepted God's will to take his son at an early age. In the host country, Mahdi had found solace through engaging in a spiritual community where he continued worshipping and trusting in God.

In contrast, Priathan's faith in God had been put to the test. Before the adversity, she was fully committed to her spiritual beliefs, but when she experienced the abuse and lost her home, she wondered why God had forsaken her and felt unworthy of his grace. She took her experience as a punishment for her lack of trust in her faith by fleeing the country and leaving her mother-in-law behind. Priathan perceived her fate through self-reproach and felt that she deserved to be punished in this way.

On this spiritual level of context, Mahdi's identity remained resilient while Priathan's belief system had been distorted by her experiences, resulting in internal spiritual conflict.

Mahdi's faith in God motivated him positively and helped stabilise his intra-psychic level through regular meditations to regulate his distress. This positive attitude also enabled him to develop and adapt a bi-cultural identity to manage the everyday societal barriers, learning the host country language and engaging in social networks. He became an active member in the community and created positive and healthy relationships, which in return helped him to advocate for his family to join him and receive the appropriate support to start the family reunion process.

In the case of Priathan, she experienced fear due to unresolved immigration status in addition to her loss of faith. She found it difficult to build relationships and presented as withdrawn and socially isolated. She feared and avoided mixed-gender community activities because some of the men who attended reminded her of those who had abused her. While Priathan was loving and caring, her experience led her to adapt an anti-social attitude in order to protect herself from a world that she no longer trusted (Easteal 1996).

On a cultural level, Mahdi felt caught between two cultures, which led to a confusion within his identity formation. On one hand, he felt committed to his traditions, but on the other hand, he recognised the need to customise himself to the host country culture in order to develop himself. After some soul searching, he felt able to identify parts of his cultural values and traditions that he wanted to retain in order to embrace both cultures simultaneously. He also appreciated some aspects of the new culture that gave him a more autonomous status.

Mahdi reflected, 'I have never cooked for myself and washed my clothes; in our country this is seen as a female role. My mother or my wife would do this willingly and in fact I would be seen as weak if I tried to help them. I now do these both roles and although initially I felt awkward, I am increasingly appreciating being self-sufficient.'

Priathan explained, 'I felt so alone when I arrived. Although my husband's sister seemed quite hostile towards me, this was overridden by my need to recreate an extended family. Living with my sister-in-law was a way to retain my culture; she often wore our traditional dress and when she did this connected me to my homeland.'

A breakdown of traditional structures can result in a collective cultural bereavement, which can impact the meanings that are shared within a family. Priathan reflected on the many years they lived happily as a family unit, when her husband had a good job and the children were doing well at school. However, Priathan had become increasingly concerned about her husband's political activism, and while she was aware that her brother and mother-in-law had asked him on many occasions not to protest against the government due to the danger it brought to the family, she was not able to express this herself. This was because even though she was fearful of the danger her husband was putting them under, her cultural conditioning as a loyal wife prevented her from going against her husband's wishes.

'I feel so angry. I cannot understand why my husband did not listen to advice and keep away from politics. He knew how much this was putting us in danger and yet nobody could stop him because he wanted to fight for justice. I have suffered so much because of his actions. I do care about him but it is now very difficult for me to feel good about him without being angry.'

It was evident that Priathan had harboured resentment towards her husband over a long time in silence and now that she was able to express this, she recognised that in her commitment to being an obedient wife she had instead internalised a victim identity. In the host country, Priathan lost the role of wife and daughter-in-law when the family dynamic changed, and this added complexity to her evolving identity. However, it also offered another viewpoint from which new identity and possibilities could emerge.

In previous chapters, we shared how Mahdi lost his son in the conflict. While we acknowledge that Mahdi was bereaved and mourned his son's loss, he had, however, found solace through his faith and his son's picture, which he treasured and carried in his pocket. This was symbolic and gave him the link he needed to be close to his son. Hence, on the family level, while Mahdi displayed low levels of depression and few symptoms of grief as a result of his resilience, he showed intense yearning for his wife and daughters who were alive but in a different country. By facing the reality of what was possible and accepting the loss of his son, it was maybe better to term this as a healthy adjustment for Mahdi, rather than pathologising it as a denial of grief.

On the level of episode, while Mahdi had gone through many traumatic events, it was the loss of his son that was the determining factor in deciding to flee the country. In the case of Priathan, it was the sexual abuse.

Priathan reflected, 'When the security forces beat and sexually abused me, I felt I was no longer a person with my own identity. I always feel dirty, I wash two times a day and I am never clean, I don't know what to do. I have tried using different soaps and perfumes but am always smelling bad. How can I tell anybody what happened to me?'

Another level of context that can impact the self-identity are the more intangible elements that are linked to a specific environment which, when left, may not be apparent. These may include climatic conditions, sounds and smells particular to a region. For Priathan, it was the seasonal food that she ate in her home country. In the host country, it was when she bought provisions in the supermarket that she noticed that certain foods were available irrespective of the season that they were grown in.

Priathan exclaimed, 'I miss going to the market. I used to go and sell our seasonal farm produce and chat with other women about the various dishes that could be made with them. Here I'm not sure what season it is as I can buy the same produce all through the year.'

For Mahdi it was the roads, as in the host country they were all tarmacked and regularly wet because of the frequent rain. Mahdi reflected, 'The air here is fresh and windy; in our country it is mostly dusty because of our roads, which have no tarmac.'

It can be disconcerting for refugees when they notice the absence of elements that had always been part of their life in their homeland. However, once the value of such elements is appreciated it can be helpful to find the actual items, such as cultural food, or symbolic representations of these in the host country. This can enhance the sense of belonging and comfort, which can be reassuring and meaningful while negotiating one's identity across two cultures (Papadopoulos 2002).

LEARNING ACTIVITIES
Think about the following:

- How do you define yourself?

- What gives your life meaning?

- What do you feel passionate about and why?

- What qualities help you when you are under pressure?

CHAPTER 6

REFUGEE TRAUMA AND MENTAL HEALTH

Not all are traumatised but all have lost their home.

Renos Papadopoulos

After reading this chapter and completing the learning activities provided, you should be able to understand:

- the most relevant categories of mental health for refugee and asylum-seeking people given their experience of the four phases

- the psychological impact, including cultural factors that may come into play while assessing the refugees' psychosocial needs

- the different concepts of mental health symptoms in relation to the refugee experience

- how to reduce the risk of mental illness and enhance wellbeing

- refugees' internal conflicts and external triggers and how symbolic events can trigger past distress.

The subject of mental health often brings many concerns. This might involve people we know who have had or been treated for mental health conditions, and it might concern our own issues.

Given that the refugee experience is likely to involve human rights abuses, the psychological impact on refugee mental health can be profound. While this can cause asylum seekers and refugees to present with mental health symptoms, this does not necessarily mean that they have mental health illness. This said, ongoing exposure to psychosocial factors, including separation from loved ones, bereavement, fear of being returned to discrimination and torture, as well as destitution in the host country, may place them at risk of developing mental illness.

For this reason, early interventions to address such issues of persecution, loss and separation can be effective in helping clients improve their wellbeing by processing their distress and developing their strengths. However, we have found, particularly with our asylum-seeking clients who have to negotiate many levels of needs concurrently, that this leaves little space and time to grieve for their losses and process their distress.

'I find it emotionally difficult to grieve for my mother-in-law when I am preoccupied with fear of being deported back to persecution. How can I have time to mourn when I do not feel safe?' Priathan reflected.

We have found that Priathan's experience of anxiety is common to many asylum seekers who, without refugee status, live in a psychological state of being too scared to recall their past given the uncertainty of their future. Similarily with Mahdi's symptoms of post-traumatic stress disorder (PTSD), we need to be aware that these could be normal responses to abnormal events, rather than pathologise these symptoms which, with the right psychosocial support, would be at less risk of developing into mental health illness.

As Mahdi and Priathan's cases illustrate, when making mental health assessments and diagnoses it is essential to include the external circumstances asylum seekers face. A mental health diagnosis of anxiety, suggesting that anxiety is an inappropriate intra-psychic reaction to a past event that is no longer dangerous, may not be the most accurate term for asylum seekers, given that being returned to persecution remains a very real danger in their future if they are not granted refugee status. We think it helpful to term this as fear, an appropriate response to danger, so as to factor in the external reality responsible for causing the internally felt distress as delineated in the four phases of refugee experience. In this context, as well as the fear of being deported back to persecution, other external causes of fear are present. These include destitution and discrimination in the host country. In addition they remain in constant risk of detention and possible exploitation.

Similarly, we should attend to the external causes of sadness refugees experience, that could develop into depression, as a factor in order to evaluate their response. First, the sadness of the loss of their home, exiled from their country and loved ones who still reside there, is common to all refugees. Other causes of sadness include imprisonment in the homeland that caused them to leave; and in the host country, isolation from not speaking the language and having reduced status in work.

These experiences of sadness and fear are identified as factors that may cause the two conditions categorised in mental health terminology as depression and anxiety, and which Moss *et al.* (2006), representatives of the World Health Organization and international authors of health monographs, discerned as most prevalent in a refugee context. For this reason, it seems essential to be aware of the external factors causal to fear and sadness before they develop into depression and anxiety.

For Priathan, the fear she had experienced during the second phase of persecution and, particularly, during the perilous journey of the third phase, reduced when she claimed asylum in the host country and was accepted as an asylum seeker. However, she realised the danger was far from over when she went to discuss her asylum case with her solicitor.

'I got back from my solicitor and felt devastated. He told me my case was not straightforward and that there was a 50 per cent chance I would be refused. Although he said he would appeal if I was refused, I felt terrified. The horrors of my persecution back home, and the shame of what I had to do to survive and escape, would become real again if I was sent back.'

Priathan realised that without refugee status she faced being returned to her homeland, and the danger of this caused her to feel great fear again. This was exacerbated by the exploitation she experienced on the journey (sadly common as fleeing refugees become vulnerable to those seeking people to traffic (Unicef 2016)). In addition she lived with the feeling of great shame as a result of the sexual abuse she had endured along the journey, which impeded her ability to integrate into a new culture causing her great sadness and leaving her feeling isolated.

Many refugees such as Priathan come from countries that have different understandings of mental health symptoms and which may lack some terminology used in the host country, including the term depression. It is therefore important to understand how they experience their distress and what interpretation and meaning they attach to this in order to offer them the appropriate support.

'I told the therapist I was suffering from persistent headache, body pains and I lacked motivation to do anything,' said Priathan. 'I also spent a lot of time in bed. She asked if I was depressed and initially I didn't understand what she meant. When she clarified it, I told her that in my culture this was seen as a spiritual ailment for which we would visit a traditional healer to perform a particular ritual to allow it to leave. She also seemed to connect my body symptoms to my mind and I found it hard to talk about my distress in this manner, fearing that I may be seen as going mad.'

Priathan's experience of therapy highlights the importance of cultural awareness. In her culture, mental health issues were taboo and, therefore, shameful to speak about. Although she suspected that two members of her community had mental health issues, this had been well hidden by their families, out of the public gaze, and Priathan was not familiar with their symptoms. When her therapist described the symptoms and meaning of depression which needed treatment, Priathan seemed unwilling to see the link to what she described as somatic pains in her body (Tribe 2002; Bhugra 2004).

It is useful to be aware that in many cultures, the mind is not seen as a separate entity from the body. For this reason, people from such cultures may express psychological distress as pain in the body, which is termed somatisation. This also means that diagnoses specifying mental health conditions such as depression, PTSD and psychosis (such as schizophrenia) have no comparable frame of reference. Consequently, there is no comparable vocabulary to express and describe symptoms, which are often seen as arising from magical or spiritual forces (Lefley 2010). It is common, for example, in some cultures, for these symptoms to be seen as evil or ancestoral spirits requiring spiritual practices to ameliorate them.

Furthermore, as well as facilitating refugees' understanding of different concepts of mental health, the style by which they are described also serves their comprehension if they are discussed in a culturally sensitive manner. This is because while people from some cultures may be able to openly express their feelings, those from other cultures need to be invited to share them – by sensitively asking open questions, for example – which could be vital in accessing the experience of their distress.

Fortunately, if putting such issues into language is problematic, there are universal features of mental health conditions that can be assessed through observation. This can be well served by making a biopsychosocial assessment of biological factors such as high blood pressure, psychological presentations, like worry, insomnia, and anorexia, and behaviour that is agitated, numb and/or inappropriate (Westermeyer 1991).

It therefore seems obvious that assessing symptoms such as anxiety and depression and holding onto an awareness of the refugee's experiences of fear and sadness can inform our response to their needs.

As Priathan reports, 'I saw a man coming towards me in the supermarket last week and I froze in terror. It was only later, when I had left and calmed down, that I realised it was his uniform that took me back to the time when the police assaulted me in my homeland. I also feel fear when I see someone in a uniform in this country, as I am terrified that they will arrest and deport me.'

The anxiety Priathan described is common in those who are traumatised, as it can be triggered by past stimuli, such as uniforms evoking those of their torturers and creating internal panic (Garcia-Peltoniemi 1991). In addition, asylum seekers live in constant fear of being apprehended and deported (Aroian 1993). This can even present as paranoia when home country persecution is triggered by host country authority institutions and authority figures (Westermeyer 1991).

Symptoms of PTSD – flashbacks by day and nightmares at night – are also common (American Psychiatric Association 2013). Mahdi knew that having been awarded refugee status he would not be returned to persecution, so he found it hard to accept the unbearable flashbacks and nightmares he continued to suffer from. He displayed many of the symptoms associated with post-traumatic stress disorder, namely: flashbacks, intrusive imagery, insomnia, hyper-vigilance and a reduced ability to deal with stress. Mahdi had flashbacks to the time he had been tortured in his home country. He had been subjected to cigarette burns to the skin and having his head pushed into a bucket of dirty water. Under interrogation he had been forced to disclose the location of government agents he had sworn secrecy to and he struggled to forgive himself for this. Mahdi also described intrusive imagery of his time in prison when he witnessed other prisoners being beaten on the soles of their feet and then blindfolded before being exposed to the sun. Also in prison at night, he heard women scream in other rooms and could only imagine what was going on, fearing his mother, wife and daughters could face the same fate. Mahdi saw these images as vividly as if he was back there reliving it. He had a reduced ability to deal with stress, he felt overwhelmed with helplessness and hopelessness and found it hard to remember things such as appointments and communications from other people. Mahdi also looked hyper-vigilant, as if he was constantly in danger, and explained that he was unable to sleep, even when he felt exhausted.

Mahdi's mental health symptoms and distress were understandable based on his lived experience. He was not able to differentiate between the symptoms of his body and his mind and was confused about how to describe them. In addition, he had a belief that a man needed to be strong and not accept defeat from his enemies.

Mahdi's case illustrates that refugee trauma needs to be understood within its own realm. It is not based on one traumatic incident but rather a continuum of experience from the apprehension stage through to the re-building and resettlement phase when refugees are fully integrated, however their past is still part of who they are. Refugee trauma can be understood as being in a state of constant fight, flight or freeze. Being in this state means that refugees are often wearing their emotional amour as a defence to protect their sanity. Refugees have lost so much in the way of tangible and intangible assets that it can be overwhelming for the brain to comprehend what could be available to them. In our work with refugees, many have shared their sense of overwhelming loss with us. One refugee reflected that he felt like a walking empty shell, while another spoke of how the loss created in him a vacuum that was impossible to fill and he could find no meaning to life.

It is no wonder that working with refugee trauma presents challenges in therapy and in other interpersonal relationships.

Mahdi reflected, 'It is impossible to identify which is the main source of my distress. It is like having many antennas all picking up different signals and ringing alarm bells with different tunes at the same time and all demanding my immediate response through my body, soul and mind.' (See Appendices B and C).

Depression – from past and current sadness

'When I got refugee status I felt less anxious but my grief overwhelmed me. I was surprised at the time, given how long I had been away from my homeland, but now it makes sense. I was so scared of being sent back to persecution that when I knew I was safe, it hit me. I suddenly knew I might never see the land of my birth again. This also made me feel very angry, and I felt ashamed at how many people I shouted at and wanted to argue with.'

Mahdi describes his grief at multiple losses. As we have observed, it is at the stage when attaining refugee status that many refugees feel safe enough to take off their emotional armour and the reality of their loss hits home. This is often accompanied by anger that, for some, is projected onto others through conflicts or, for others, is internalised and can lead to depression (Arredondo-Dowd 1981). Mahdi also felt angry, betrayed and resentful towards his country's government because they failed to protect the country from the rebels who tortured him, and hence he felt ambivalent towards the host country.

'My confidence was knocked. I had no one to support me from home, and in the host country even though I had been learning the language I could not yet speak it well enough to get a job. I was very successful in my homeland but here I felt like a complete failure.'

Mahdi's experience of having lower self-esteem from a reduced social status is a frequent reality. Often, due to the language barrier, those with high professional qualifications and experience have to find work that only needs basic language skills, such as jobs that primarily require manual labour. Additionally, for men, changed gender roles can be challenging. Often, women previously not allowed to work in their culture have to work because the men cannot get a job and become the breadwinners (Ben-Porath 1991). There may also be deprivation due to limited choice from living on a bare minimum. All of these, as well as the overwhelming loss of their home and family, are causes of great sadness.

As the cumulative impact of multiple losses, isolation and low self-esteem may result in depression, it is vital first to identify them and then address each in turn, as we shall describe in detail in Part 2 of this book.

It is also important for those working with refugee people to be aware that depression may be somatised rather than verbalised, and so to look for the signs of depression in the body and through behaviour as described earlier. This is particularly important given that untreated depression may lead to suicidal ideation (NHS Choices 2017).

In the following example, we will show how understanding Priathan's cultural context and the impact of the phases of refugee experience enabled Jane, her doctor, to refer her to appropriate care.

Priathan visited the doctor for the first time in the host country because she was suffering from chest and abdominal pains as well as persistent headaches. Additionally, her skin felt irritable and scratchy. She also told the doctor that she sometimes felt dizzy. After a detailed medical assessment, the doctor asked if she was worried or not sleeping well. Priathan responded that she had not slept well since her mother-in-law died a month ago. Based on her symptoms, the doctor prescribed sleeping pills and medication to reduce her anxiety, which Priathan took diligently. The doctor also sent her for a comprehensive blood test.

On her next visit to the doctor, the blood tests had come back negative with no indication of any illness. Priathan did not understand how the doctor had no physical explanation for her symptoms. The doctor explained that they may be 'medically unexplained symptoms' which she described as physical pains in the body with no discernable medical cause that are attributed to psychological concerns (Henningsen *et al.* 2003).

While Priathan remained confused, when her somatic symptoms and nightmares persisted she returned to see her doctor. When Priathan described sleep disturbances, in which her mother-in-law appeared angry with her in her dreams, the doctor sought to gain a better understanding by using a biopsychosocial approach that had a culturally sensitive component (Engel 1977). From the content of Priathan's dream, the doctor wondered if her angry mother-in-law was a manifestation of the trauma that Priathan experienced in her body which her mind had suppressed to protect her. As Priathan's blood results had come back negative, the doctor felt that medicalising her issues would not be the best approach and instead referred Priathan for talking therapy to allow her to reframe her presenting issues through a psychosocial perspective.

Priathan explained to the therapist that in her culture when family members who died appear in your dreams it is an indicator that there are unresolved issues with them. In her homeland, Priathan's grandfather had taken such cases to a traditional healer who carried out a cleansing ritual using herbal roots to honour and calm the angry spirits.

Priathan believed that this was what she needed to do; however, she did not know anyone in the host country she could consult or trust enough to ask for help. This prevented her from resolving the issues she had with her mother-in-law that caused her to feel extremely sad. We will explore how Priathan deals with this in the next part of the book.

As well as the sadness that comes from the loss of family members which frequently presents as low mood and results in social isolation, Priathan was preoccupied with the very real fear of being returned to persecution in her country which exacerbated her symptoms of PTSD. This caused her body to react to stimuli in the present that evoked past events of trauma and triggered a fight, flight or freeze response.

These symptoms can be understood as normal reactions to abnormal and devastating events. However, practitioners need to bear in mind that the way these symptoms are interpreted and the meaning given to them differ on a case by case basis. Therefore, it is important to be culturally sensitive by checking with each client what meaning they attribute their symptoms to, while remaining mindful of our own prejudice.

Other factors that impact on refugee mental health include social and cultural norms around sexual orientation. For example, in countries where being heterosexual is the only recognised and accepted gender role, those who are in same-sex relationships are socially condemned and may be physically punished in public as a warning. These human rights violations can force people who are homosexual to get married against their wish, or to create a mask that conforms to their cultural norms, which can have a profoundly detrimental effect on their mental health.

Having this understanding of refugee mental health can help us to formulate a working framework that is cultural and gender sensitive in responding to their needs, as we will explore in Part 2 of this handbook.

LEARNING ACTIVITIES

Think of someone you know who has mental health concerns.

- How easy is it for you to discuss those concerns with them?

- How are mental health issues dealt with in your family?

PART 2

THREE CORE PRINCIPLES

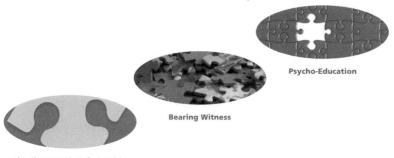

Psycho-Education

Bearing Witness

The Therapeutic Relationship

The best ways to find yourself is to lose yourself in the service of others.

Mahatma Gandhi

In Part 1 of this book we discussed the context and the issues refugees have to face. We started with the four phases of refugee experience, the separation and loss of their homeland and the challenges on arrival in the host country. We then mapped these as multiple levels of needs, explaining how these impact self-identity. By illustrating these with the case studies of Priathan, Mahdi and Arufat we hope we have helped to bring these issues – that all asylum-seeking and refugee people face – to life.

In Part 2, we will show how we worked with Priathan, Mahdi and Arufat to demonstrate the way we address the issues and meet the many needs refugees have. We do this by employing what we call three core principles: the therapeutic relationship, bearing witness and psychoeducation. It is essential to note that these three core principles work in conjunction with each other, although each has a particular role. We begin with the therapeutic relationship and nurture this throughout our work together, providing each asylum-seeking person with an environment of non-judgemental acceptance to foster their trust. Once a trusting relationship is established we bear witness to their narrative with the purpose of empathically understanding their deepest concerns. From this we identify areas in which we can empower and share useful information through psychoeducation.

While we appreciate that service providers will not be able to offer what we are able to as a therapeutic service, we hope that our learning and the model that we use will be useful in informing a way of working with refugees that can enhance their service delivery.

We will now explore each principle in turn, starting with the therapeutic relationship.

Part 2 of this book is divided into three chapters:

Chapter 7: The Therapeutic Relationship. Building a trusting relationship in which the client feels safe and accepted.

Chapter 8: Bearing Witness. Allowing the client to tell their story and understanding it from their point of reference.

Chapter 9: Psychoeducation. Offering both practical and psychological information to widen the client's choices in order to meet their needs.

▨▨ CHAPTER 7 ▨▨

THE THERAPEUTIC RELATIONSHIP

The most basic of all human needs is the need to understand and be understood. The best way to understand people is to listen to them.

Ralph Nichols

After reading this chapter and completing the learning activities provided you should be able to:

- establish a therapeutic relationship based on Rogers' core conditions of empathy, unconditional positive regard and congruence

- understand a way of embodying a hospitality attitude that is culturally sensitive

- have an awareness of the totality of the person through a biopsychosocial lens for effective interventions.

The therapeutic relationship

At the beginning of the working partnership between the refugee and the practitioner, it is essential that the service user feels safe and comfortable in order to fully explore and review their life and experience. To create the best conditions for this, it's important to provide a physical environment that is both safe and confidential – a space where they know they cannot be overheard and in which they are positioned within a familiar setting where they can leave at any time. Then the practitioner needs to introduce themselves and check how the refugee would like to be addressed, followed by information about confidentiality and its limits within the agency and how this would be breached in cases where they disclose something that would endanger their own or another's safety. It is important that the refugee is aware of what the service offers and that a collaborative discussion takes place about the refugee's hopes and expectations of it, including what they might want to achieve through working together, as well as how to complain if they have any concerns.

Many refugees will have experienced or witnessed conflict and may have been exposed to extreme violence in their homeland and on the journey to safety. As such they may not have been respected as a person of equal value and may feel their lives lack significance or even meaningless. This makes the working partnership between practitioner and refugee even more significant, because, done well, it enables a therapeutic dimension in which a reparative relationship can develop. Here, a 'non-directive' approach is important, where the practitioner encourages the client to talk freely enabling the refugee to feel accepted and respected in all their humanity.

The working client space says a lot in informing the refugee that they are welcomed in this environment. This includes how they are greeted and made comfortable, which demonstrates the practitioner's care and respect for the refugee.

Checking how they would like to be known includes asking them how to pronounce their name. As refugees' names frequently come from a different alphabetic construction that may have a different pronunciation from our own, so it's important to find a way to say their name accurately. The consequences of not doing so can be detrimental to fostering a good working relationship, as the following example illustrates.

'My key worker has never pronounced my name correctly,' says one refugee. 'The first time this happened I explained how we pronounce my name in my country in the hope that he would say it correctly. My name has a meaning in my country and, when he doesn't pronounce it in this way, it feels as though he is taking away this meaning.'

Regarding confidentiality, it's important to underline that this has two aspects. The first is the *limitations of confidentiality*. For most agencies, confidentiality is kept within their service, which means that a number of the practitioner's colleagues will also have access to the client's file. The second aspect is the *exceptions to confidentiality:* i.e. if it was felt that the client was at risk of harming themselves or others, the appropriate authorities would need to be informed. We would explain to the refugee that they would be consulted before their confidentiality was broken, if at all possible.

Risk assessment

FOR ALL LEVELS, CREATE A COLLABORATIVE PLAN
OF THE CLIENT'S GOALS, HOPES AND ASPIRATIONS
FOR THEIR FUTURE, TO ENHANCE THEIR SAFETY

Figure 7.1: Levels of risk assessment

At the start of our working partnership, it's essential to assess if the client is at risk in order to identify their immediate needs. For example, if their safety needs have been compromised now or in the past, this may trigger symptoms of anxiety in any new relationship. Their essential need for safety can also be compromised if they hear that their asylum claim has been refused, or if they are facing destitution or homelessness. In such cases, it is important to ensure that they have access to specialist services that can provide legal advice and shelter respectively. As well as external factors – i.e. challenges they are facing in the physical world – their safety may feel compromised internally due to psychological distress as a result of past traumatic experiences in their home country and on the journey to exile. This psychological distress may produce an intra-psychic experience of danger that feels as real as if it were actually happening.

As these factors may increase the client's distress and lead to suicidal ideation, it is essential to make a risk assessment before other work is undertaken. A client at risk of external or internal factors would most likely jeopardise any meaningful engagement of service and hence we encourage practitioners to be mindful of the risk factors. This may involve checking through the client's narrative if it is not coherent or observing body language for signs of self-harm. In addition, the practitioner may have concerns about the client's lifestyle or social interactions, which could be indicated by discrepancies in what they say and how they behave and any other significant symptoms.

If the client is at high risk, they may be beyond a practitioner's service remit and require referral to another specialist agency that can respond appropriately.

The manner and accuracy by which they feel heard by the practitioner will inform the level of safety they experience, and the depth to which they can share their concerns.

This comes from the practitioner's ability to work in an empathic and genuine way within the therapeutic relationship. As well as using a common language – and so ensuring that both parties can understand each other – the practitioner also needs to be informed through observation, for example by the client's *non-verbal communication of body language, tone of voice and facial expression*. It is important to be aware that although a lack of eye contact and closed body language may be a sign of reluctance to participate, it may also be a sign of respect in some cultures. It's therefore essential to always seek clarity directly from the client as to what this means for them.

In addition, the physiological responses, temperament, difference and diversity involving age, culture, race, disability, gender and social class are significant in relationships and need to be both discussed and understood for the purpose of clarifying roles. For example, a refugee who is considerably older than the practitioner may relate to them as a parent does to a child. If this is not clarified, the refugee may adopt a parental role – one that seeks to 'look after' the practitioner. This may cause the refugee to withhold rather than disclose their own needs and vulnerabilities which, in turn, would prevent them from receiving the full benefits offered by the service.

By creating this boundaried structure – working safely with a defined purpose, employing listening skills to facilitate trust and acknowledging difference – the client's narrative is able to emerge in an authentic manner. Having established this structure, as refugees come from abroad and in most cases have not been to our country before, we also underpin the therapeutic relationship with what we call a 'hospitality attitude'.

Hospitality attitude

A hospitality attitude is fostered when we imagine what it would be like for us to receive a guest from abroad who is visiting our country for the first time. For example, it may present challenges when the guest speaks a different language and follows different cultural practices. We might, therefore, need to prepare for issues with which we may be unfamiliar.

While we may mentally prepare ourselves to act as host, it's our *attitude* we want to emphasise in our working partnership with asylum seekers and refugees, as this facilitates our ability to collaborate effectively with them. The hospitality attitude places the responsibility on the host to facilitate the environment in which the therapeutic relationship can be effectively constructed.

We will seek to illustrate this hospitality attitude through the case study below.

AN EXCHANGE STUDENT CASE STUDY

Through a programme in their son's school, Maria and Peter hosted a 19-year-old exchange student called John for three months. Although Maria and Peter had acted as hosts to family and friends previously, this felt different as John was visiting their country for the first time and did not speak the same language. Maria and Peter did not know much about John or what his needs would be. They were also aware of the language barrier between them, which they were concerned could hamper their relationship. For this reason, Peter bought a basic translation book and Maria went to a local language school to ask if they had a student from John's country who would be willing to help in case they needed more urgent face-to-face translation. Peter and Maria also bought John a one-week travel card, taught him how to use the local transport system independently and gave him information on who to contact in an emergency. Anticipating that during the three months John may feel homesick, Peter researched some traditional recipes from John's homeland in the hope that he would feel more at home if he ate food to which he was accustomed.

As a result, John expressed how he was able to quickly engage with his hosts, 'I had been a bit worried about spending such a long time with people I did not know, especially because I could not communicate with them in their own language. However, they made such an effort to understand me and to explain what I needed to know that I soon felt relaxed. Peter had even made the effort of cooking one of my country's favourite dishes; as I ate it I closed my eyes and felt as if I was back home.'

We hope that this demonstrates how adopting a hospitality attitude can create an immediate bond with someone from a different culture who is unfamiliar to us. In the case of refugees, there may be a fundamental problem of trust given their context of persecution, in which most of them may have been exposed to different types of violence and/or abuse by the people in whom they put their faith, as was the case for Priathan.

Priathan

Priathan was referred to a therapist for counselling by her doctor after she had complained of sleep disturbances and panic attacks.

When Priathan came to see the therapist for the first time, the therapist introduced herself, and after talking about what counselling entailed she also explained in detail about the confidentiality of the service and the two exceptional reasons why this confidentiality might be breached. Priathan found it difficult to accept and appeared sceptical about this information guaranteeing confidentiality.

'I have lost trust in humanity, I no longer have any privacy and my dignity has been abused many times by people I have put my trust in. I don't know if I can trust you.'

We appreciate that not all disciplines negotiate confidentiality directly with the client; however, it is an ethical and legal requirement that all practitioners follow data-protective principles.

The therapist empathised and reflected back to Priathan an understanding of her concerns around trusting other people based on her past experiences. She further showed her willingness to work with these concerns and to review their working relationship when they needed to. The therapist also acknowledged the difference in their cultures and having come from different backgrounds with different life experiences. To manage this difference she offered to check for clarity with Priathan the interpretation she gave to her experiences to ensure she was being understood within her own frame of reference. Priathan nodded and felt reassured when she heard this. The tension in her face appeared to ease and she was then able to focus internally on her concerns.

When refugees have had their human rights abused and trust broken by significant others, it is understandable that they may lack trust in others and see the world as a dangerous place. For this reason, while embodying a hospitality attitude is valuable, it is essential that we offer an effective method where we connect to the refugee on an equal and human level. We have found that applying Rogers' (1957) core conditions of acceptance, empathy and congruence provides a powerful framework to facilitate such an equal connection in developing and establishing a working relationship.

The core conditions: acceptance, empathy and congruence

Given that oppression, rejection and suppression are much in evidence in a refugee context of persecution, we suggest that each of these core conditions has significant value. For this reason, we will explore the value of each, starting with acceptance.

Acceptance is an attitude of non-judgement which underpins the whole process. This provides the refugee with an environment in which they feel free to express themselves without censure.

Empathy seeks to understand the other person's subjective frame of reference. It is demonstrable in that a person will know they are being profoundly listened to and understood if an accurate representation of what they are experiencing is reflected back to them. Employing an attitude of hospitality also enables the therapist to have an open mind and understand the client from their internal frame of reference. It's essential to appreciate their experience, as if walking in their shoes, while also having the capacity to step in and step out of them so as not to lose oneself in this process.

Congruence ensures that, while the refugee is free to express themselves without being judged, the therapist is able to offer reflection when discrepancies appear in their story. If the refugee acknowledges this disparity, it is likely that trust will develop in the therapist–refugee relationship, as there will be an understanding on both sides that the other person is genuine.

'When I went to talk to the therapist I was worried about talking about what happened to me,' said Priathan. 'I had managed to tell my solicitor the facts of my abuse, but, as a consequence, the feelings I had of shame felt overwhelming. I was scared that I would not be able to talk at all, and just remain frozen under the weight of the violent events I had experienced at home and on my journey.'

In the first session, after agreeing confidentiality, Priathan became quiet and tearful. She sat there for a while and looked at the therapist with sadness in her eyes; she seemed to be in a lot of emotional distress. The therapist held her gaze warmly with open body language to give her space and reassure her that she was safe. After some silence, Priathan began to speak softly and at times the therapist could hardly hear her voice; it seemed as though Priathan was fading in front of her, so the therapist sat closer and mirrored her faint voice. This helped Priathan to recognise that it was hard for the therapist to hear her and she began to speak more clearly to connect with her.

The therapist's role in the initial sessions is to create an environment in which a therapeutic relationship can be established. In Priathan's case, by embodying the core conditions, the therapist provided her with a warm, safe and non-judgemental space in which she connected empathically by walking at Priathan's pace and in the direction that she chose to go. Realising she was being non-judgementally accepted, Priathan felt increasingly safe and stable and began to develop trust in the process.

In the following sessions, the empathic understanding of the therapist meant that Priathan was able to accept what had happened to her and fully articulate the shame she felt without feeling judged. The therapist noted a feeling of despair when Priathan talked about the sexual violence she had experienced on the journey in a very calm, matter of fact manner. She reflected to Priathan this feeling of despair evoked by her narrative. In doing so, the therapist was being congruent with her feelings, which she then offered to Priathan to consider or reflect on.

'It was really hard to hear the therapist reflecting back to me the despair I felt I had,' said Priathan. 'I thought I had hidden this feeling – and the guilt I carried – deep inside me. Over the next week, I initially struggled to contain the guilt and waves of shame that it brought back. Then, because the truth had been brought into the light, I began to look at what it meant to me and was able to discover things I had not been able to see before.'

Priathan believed that she had 'consented' to the smugglers because she did not protest against the sexual abuse towards her. The smugglers were also doing her a favour helping her to flee to safety. This placed a burden of self-blame on her which evoked shame and social stigma. She also felt guilt for feeling grateful towards the smugglers who had brought her to safety.

While Priathan knew that she was powerless to stop the government agents from their acts of abuse in her homeland, she found it hard to believe she had no other choice with the people smugglers.

The therapist checked with Priathan and wondered what she could have done with the people smugglers that would have had a different outcome.

This enabled Priathan to explore the extent to which she could have said 'no'. In doing so, she was able to appreciate that although she could have protested she believed that, at the time, her own survival, and that of her children, would have been compromised to an unacceptable degree.

The trust that this engendered between her and the therapist allowed Priathan to address causal factors that preceded the events of her persecution and subsequent journey. This involved her upbringing as a woman in a shame-based culture. In confronting this, she began to realise that her cultural context had added significant weight to the already sizeable amount of shame she carried.

The core conditions were the process by which Priathan was able to free herself from her cultural conditioning: what Rogers describes as 'conditions of worth' (1959). In discerning these, a person is able to realise that who they *really are* is conflicting with this conditioning, and thus determines who they think they *have to be*. As such, they have an opportunity to choose to be congruent and can let this falsehood go.

As this example illustrates, establishing a safe and nurturing therapeutic relationship creates the foundation on which the practitioner is able to facilitate interventions that can both contain distress and encourage development within the other person.

As we identified in Chapter 4, refugees present with multiple and complex needs which demand a holistic response in order to attend to the totality of the person. For asylum seekers and refugees there are also social and cultural factors that are essential to bear in mind in order to make effective interventions. All these elements are interlinked. We have found that Engel's (1977) biopsychosocial model provides an appropriate and helpful way to respond to the needs of this group.

Biopsychosocial assessment

The understanding of the refugee experience as described in Part 1 of this handbook is essential in informing us of the refugee's multiple levels of complex needs, which often occur simultaneously in a refugee context which can detrimentally impact their wellbeing. This is why a multidimensional approach is needed to provide a holistic response.

Because of this, we have found that applying a biopsychosocial assessment helps to identify the client's health, psychological, social and practical needs. We believe using this assessment whatever the service you are providing is essential in bringing awareness of the refugee's other needs which may impact on the effectiveness of delivering your service. By doing so, the practitioner can actively engage the refugee in encouraging them to access other useful services to meet their holistic needs.

This assessment encompasses the biological aspect of the person which may need medical attention to address issues such as: actual body pains, breathing difficulties, physical injuries, illness, TB, HIV, excess sweating, etc. The practitioner checks with the client how they are feeling here and now to ensure the client is accessing the necessary health treatment.

Then we have the psychological aspect to assess the emotional wellbeing and, in particular, pay attention to any symptoms that may hinder the client's ability to engage with the service. It's important to listen to the client's narrative and their interpretation of their experiences as this will inform how they engage with the service. If the client is a torture survivor, it is essential to offer them a referral to long term rehabilitation programme for torture survivors. In cases where the client shares their loss and separation from family members, we have found that using McGoldrick and Gerson 1985 genogram to be an effective way in bringing cognition of the client's family status which can help to put their loss and separation into perspective. This can also contribute to the commencement of the grieving process as well as accepting the reality of the loss. A *genogram* is a graphic chart of a family which shows relationships and how one is situated in the family. In the refugee context this chart highlights members who are alive, dead or missing.

The third aspect is the social aspect which involves checking food, shelter and clothing. Other significant social aspects include the wider social links and cultural connections, how well they are adapting to the local culture which enhance their sense of belonging and their immigration status which is key to their feelings of safety. Social needs are a priority after the biological needs, without these the client may not be able to engage in higher level.This is the psychological level which includes self esteem and self actualisation.

Levels	Negative effects			Neutral effects	Positive effects
	INJURY, WOUND				
	Psychiatric disorders (PD), PTSD	Distressful psychological reactions (DPR)	Ordinary human suffering (OHS)	RESILIENCE	ADVERSITY-ACTIVATED DEVELOPMENT (AAD)
Individual					
Family					
Community					
Society/culture					

Figure 7.2: Intense Adversity Trauma Grid

While refugees often focus on trauma in their narrative, which is consistent with the trauma discourse that is dominant in the media and society at large. It is important to be aware that this is only one facet of their totality and that, albeit an important one, they also have other facets which often are suppressed by this dominant story of trauma.

We have found the Papadopoulos's (2007) Adversity-Trauma Grid to be useful in providing a framework to identify not only the client's vulnerability but also to account for their strengths as well as their new strengths and skills they have developed as a result of their exposure to adversity; these new strengths that did not exist before the adversity Papadopoulos termed 'Adversity Activated development' (AAD). The Adversity-Trauma grid framework highlights what Papadopoulos calls the 'complexity, uniqueness, and totality' (CUT) of the multiple levels of contexts that govern these situations. Therefore, the Grid includes not only the negative effects of being exposed to adversity, but also the positive ones, as well as those responses that remained unchanged. It highlights the reality that whilst refugees may have traumatic experiences as a result of their exposure to adversity, at the same time, they also retain some strengths as well as they learn from their adversity and develop new positive responses that they did not have previously. We found this framework most useful for our work. It helps us to perceive the complexity of the refugees and their situations and prevents us from falling into oversimplified formulas that emphasise the trauma exclusively.

For example, while Priathan presented as vulnerable and dependent due to past experiences, it was evident that she had innate strengths that helped her make difficult decisions to save herself and her daughters bringing them through the journey to exile. Coming from a traditional structure of patriarchy and traditional gender roles she had started to identify and appreciate her autonomy and feel liberated in the host country. She discovered that she was capable of being a breadwinner for her children, and employ her cooking skills in a career to facilitate this. In her homeland this would have been perceived as rebellious as such activities were deemed socially and culturally unacceptable.

In Arufat's case, he presented himself as vulnerable due to the adversity and his overwhelming loss and separation of family, in addition he has lost his leg and a career as a doctor. Before adversity Arufat had everything he needed in life, he held himself of high status expecting others to serve him. After the adversity he had to survive without his wife, who had done most of the housework that included cooking for him. He gradually started to appreciate his autonomy in doing things for himself in a positive way. He also discovered he had great leadership skills to encourage others in similar situation.

For Mahdi he was not a political activist however through adversity, he had discovered his passion and voice to campaign on social media against the abuse in his home country.

So as part of the assessment, we identify positive factors in order to get a more holistic appreciation of the client, who will also be able to reflect on and tap into the resources that they have in order to flourish and enhance their ability to cope.

The practitioner's impression gained through observing the refugee's body language, the coherence of the narrative and level of dissociation also informs the assessment. From this, actions can be made to ensure that the refugee is provided with the right support to enable them to articulate their needs to service providers who are able to meet them. Rogers' (1959) core conditions of empathy, acceptance and congruence, which we discussed earlier, are central to this assessment process to ensure that the refugee stays at the heart of the work.

Having established an effective therapeutic relationship and completed a biopsychosocial assessment to identify their presenting needs, we will now consider how to bear witness to their narrative.

LEARNING ACTIVITIES

Reflect on two people in your life. One that you have a strong relationship with called A and the second called B that you struggle to relate to.

- What values do you share that help to create a strong relationship with A?

- What values do you need to develop in order to build a stronger relationship with B?

- What have you learnt about yourself after reading this chapter?

CHAPTER 8

BEARING WITNESS

In the middle of difficulty lies opportunity.

Albert Einstein

After reading this chapter and completing the learning activities you will understand the importance of:

- the culture being both a hindrance and a support for the refugee

- cultural humility and being culturally sensitive

- being psychologically resilient in order to allow the client to express their distress.

We have found that if we are able to establish a trusting relationship, our refugee clients feel safe enough to connect with and share their concerns with us that we bear witness to.

Five psychosocial dimensions

When bearing witness to a refugee, we consider five psychosocial levels of context within which they are situated due to the impact that they will have on our work together. The levels are socio-political (their asylum claim), cultural (their own culture as well as that of the host country and organisations within it), interpersonal (relationship between the refugee and practitioner), intra-psychic in terms of the refugee, and intra-psychic in terms of the practitioner.

On an intra-psychic level in a refugee context where persecution and even torture have been used, we suggest that it is crucial that a practitioner carefully monitors their own intra-psychic experience so that their non-directive approach is not compromised by relating in a detached, or conversely, intrusive manner (Pope and Garcia-Peltoniemi 1991); for example, by noting experiences of discomfort that may create distance, so as not to have to go with the refugee into their distressing material, or, contrarily, to satisfy their own voyeuristic interest, by asking them to reflect in greater detail on the material than they may want to.

On an interpersonal level, it is also important to be sensitive about only being non-directive: as Afuape (2011, p.103) explains, 'This may be experienced as disinterest', as many refugees have 'lost a significant proportion of their intimate relationships'. It may therefore be helpful to make the relationship more personal in a professional way. While relating as an equal it is important to offer one's professional expertise if a refugee requires it (Madsen 1999). For example, if a refugee is feeling suicidal, it is vital to make a comprehensive risk assessment. In this way, a practitioner will be able to provide a protective responsibility when a refugee is at risk; and a responsibility to the refugee, to help them facilitate their own preferred meanings, when they are safe enough. This is how we suggest a practitioner would best serve their refugee client: by relating as an expert on one side of a spectrum that has the position of an entirely collaborative equal on the other (Madsen 2007).

On the cultural level of the host country's laws and policy, a practitioner does need to be an expert in the entitlements that the refugee person may otherwise be unaware of, and offer or refer them to organisations who can ensure that their basic needs of health, food and shelter are met (Maslow 1943). We provide Engel's (1977) biopsychosocial assessment to ensure that the refugee has this foundation of care beneath them. Once these are in place we are then able to bear witness to their intra-psychic meaning in a non-directive manner.

As bearing witness requires travelling with a refugee to wherever they wish to go, we suggest that to do this, it is essential that the practitioner has a good understanding of the different themes that refugees present with as highlighted in Part 1 of this book: loss and separation, acculturation, multiple levels of needs, self-identity and refugee mental health.

Bearing in mind that while most refugees would have been through and witnessed traumatic events, this does not necessarily mean they have been traumatised. Papadopoulos (2007) explains that it is therefore essential that practitioners also pay attention to the refugees' strength and resilience as well as their trauma.

By bearing witness with an awareness of the totality of all of these factors we have found that it is possible to respond to events that may be beyond our comprehension, such as a refugee's multiple losses of home and loved ones, in a congruent manner. To do this, we suggest, a practitioner needs to provide the right level of connection between neither being too distant, risking alienating the refugee further, nor over supportive, which could disempower and revictimise them.

In addition, as the refugee experience often involves harrowing experiences of persecution it is important to be aware of the challenges to, as well as the importance of, bearing witness to them. Blackwell (1997), in describing bearing witness to torture survivors, stresses the danger in seeking to 'help' a client to feel better (such as by doing things for them) rather than (which he asserts is necessary) allow them to express often unimaginable and overwhelming accounts of their persecution that is likely to make them feel worse. To facilitate this process, Blackwell discusses the value of Winnicott's (1953, 1971) concept of 'holding' through emotional understanding, and Bion's (1959, 1962) 'containing' of often unbearable projected feelings. These theories also inform our work for which we liken the practitioner to a vessel – a sea-going ship that has a stabilising keel to hold and strong hull to contain, within which the refugee can feel safe when experiencing even the worst emotional weather.

As the expression 'an even keel' states, the keel represents the stability that the practitioner needs to provide for the refugee to stand on in order to feel safe while holding the often-considerable weight of their concerns. To do this, the practitioner needs to be clear of any emotional distress in their own psychological structure that could compromise their integrity and destabilise them. This distress may be due to unresolved issues such as personal losses or experiences of abuse that can be triggered by similar material that their client brings.

The hull of the vessel represents the strength that the practitioner also needs, not only to withstand but also to empathically connect to their client's emotional weather. This could include violent storms, from flashbacks to persecution that may have involved torture, as well as periods of inactivity in the doldrums, from an internal state of helplessness caused by events such as imprisonment.

If the keel is stable and the hull strong enough to keep them both safe, the practitioner will then be able to invite their client within and give them captaincy to steer this vessel to the places that they need to go to. In so doing, the practitioner will be able to bear witness to the full range of their client's emotional experience. By empathically experiencing the often crushing weight of these waves of emotion directly, the practitioner is then able to reflect the experience and feelings that were present for them back to their client, modulated in a way that will not destabilise them. If the refugee experiences this as an accurate account of what they were going through at the time, they may be able to reclaim them as their own. By putting words to their experience, the refugee has an opportunity to re-author and regroup the missing links, which may have become disconnected from their story, and express them in a narrative that enables their meaning to emerge.

To facilitate this, we use White's (1990) Narrative Therapy which describes how the dominant story, the one that is most told, becomes accepted as a standard of normality of 'truth' against which any other story is, therefore, subjugated in comparison. As we have found that so many refugees have subjugated values that they prize beneath a dominant story of persecution, when bearing witness we employ this approach to identify these stories within our clients' narrative. Developing a narrative that is true to their own values can result in an experience of empowerment by which refugees regain greater control over their lives as, we hope, the following examples with Arufat and Priathan illustrate.

Arufat first came for therapy two months after he had arrived in the host country having lost his right leg when a bomb planted in his car exploded while he was driving to work.

At the beginning of the session the therapist observed that Arufat seemed to be gazing into the distance unable to focus on anything, his body was slumped and he appeared deflated. When it was reflected back to him that his body was hunched over, Arufat looked up before bending his head down again. The therapist allowed him space to connect with his process and after some minutes of reflection Arufat said, almost inaudibly, 'There is nothing I can do.' The therapist felt that the room was filled with sadness and offered this to Arufat, who nodded slowly, became tearful and sighed heavily, 'My life is all over, there is nothing to live for.'

The therapist paraphrased this, 'It sounds as if you are feeling hopeless, as if there is no point in living' and Arufat looked up stating, 'I had everything I needed, but when I lost my leg that was the point I lost everything.' Arufat said this in a heavy and conclusive manner. He seemed to have decided that from the moment he lost his leg, there was nothing more for him to contribute in life. In the next two sessions, Arufat further reflected on his loss of purpose from not being able to be a political activist, to the loss of his medical practice and, mostly, that he could no longer provide for his family, from which he experienced the loss of his masculinity as a provider.

Arufat's dominant story was that the loss of his leg was the cause of the loss of everything else – his country, livelihood, family, dignity and masculinity. He presented himself as a victim and had spent many months blaming himself for failing his family and being a coward for fleeing the country. From this narrative of failure Arufat felt hopeless, powerless and guilty; he saw little purpose to his life.

The therapist offered an accurate reflection of Arufat's experience and validation of his feelings, without sympathising or rescuing him, which allowed Arufat to feel increasingly safe to connect with the full extent of his distress.

In doing so, Arufat experienced that, in so many months in which he had felt powerless, here he had full autonomy to choose to go where he needed to. Arufat was able to explore all the aspects of his loss during each session and reflect on these throughout the rest of the week. He found that he was able to check his interpretation of events against what had happened by going back to the actual time of the event. Arufat expressed that he had been determined to stay and help treat the injured and sick people of his community. He spoke movingly, comparing himself with the people who had lost their lives fighting for the country. Through this Arufat was able to look at the judgement of survival guilt that he believed he deserved for leaving the conflict. He also considered what he could have done if he had stayed and been unable to continue working without one leg due to the lack of specialist treatment. Arufat was able to grieve the loss of those people who shared his purpose and appreciate that by surviving he remained a living witness to the sacrifice they had made.

In the following session Arufat appeared lighter and more upright, as if a weight had been lifted from his shoulders. He explained that during the week he recognised that, by being alive, he could tell others about the sacrifice of those he had fought with and the cause that they had died for. When the therapist reflected the courage and strength that Arufat described them to have he also acknowledged his own. He also said that he had reflected that with one leg, had he stayed to protest, he would probably have been able to do little to help, whereas here he could continue by giving his testimony through social media and at rallies. Arufat also realised that the main reason that he was alive was due to the leg that he had lost; that losing his leg may have actually *saved* his life. He began to be thankful that he had lost his leg and find comfort in the possibility of meeting his family again. Through bearing witness, Arufat was able to recreate himself through multiple narratives and identify with the one that was most meaningful to him (Myerhoff 1986). With his new-found hope, he was able to focus on the possibilities of what he had, rather than what he had lost, which marked a new chapter for Arufat (Eastmond 1989).

For Arufat, his dominant story had been one of a coward and a failure who had left the cause when he lost his leg, which also meant that he was unable to fulfil the role of a man who provided for his family. Bearing witness to this enabled Arufat to see the subjugated story underneath, of a survivor who had stood up against oppression, who would now continue to do so through the media, and find other ways to provide for his wife and children.

For Priathan, her dominant story was of shame, due to the judgement of her home culture that it was the responsibility of the woman to remain pure, which compounded her traumatised psychological response to her rape by the police in her homeland and the people smugglers on the journey to the host country. This made it difficult for Priathan to speak about what had happened and so prevented her from processing her shame.

The therapist invited Priathan to explore the meaning she gave to her feelings of shame and guilt, which allowed Priathan to reflect on what these meant in her cultural context. Before she had started to work with the therapist, Priathan had seen her doctor on a regular basis, complaining of feeling hot, dizzy and short of breath. This had become so severe that she feared she was going to die and leave her children as orphans. It was at this point that her doctor referred her for counselling. In her country, Priathan would have confided her concerns to her mother and had never confided to a stranger. She therefore had initially not seen the benefit of speaking to a stranger and feared openly talking about the overwhelming feelings she was experiencing. However, due to her distress she decided to try what was on offer. She admitted that having done so was a huge relief because the therapist allowed her a safe space where she was able to express her concerns.

In subsequent sessions, Priathan reflected how the government agents 'tore her clothes' while her children were forced to stay in the next room. She further stated she had not done anything to deserve such cruelty, which concurs with Crawley (2001) who suggests that in some cases, women are subjected to human rights violations simply because they are mothers, wives and daughters of people whom the authorities consider to be 'dangerous' or 'undesirable'. When the therapist invited her to share more about how her clothes were torn, Priathan retorted dismissively that it was 'OK' and that her clothes were 'not that important'. As she spoke, the therapist noted a heaviness in her tone and wondered if Priathan was attempting to minimise the event. The therapist was aware of Priathan's cultural norms around topics that were considered taboo to speak about, such as sexual violence and rape. The stigma associated with such issues could bring shame and dishonour to her family and the risk of being socially ostracised by the community. The therapist considered whether Priathan's dismissive manner might be a way to protect herself from remembering such traumatic events and her fear of the consequences of their disclosure on her family. The therapist was concerned about the possible negative impact that such past experiences of distress could have in forming secure relationships and the challenge this could present to their working relationship.

While Priathan did not seem prepared to speak about 'how her clothes were torn', she had been able to express her anger towards her husband for putting the family at risk. She experienced this as a betrayal of his commitment to protect her and blamed him for failing their family. After saying this Priathan suddenly looked confused, she lowered her voice and apologised for getting angry. Priathan then spoke about her love for her husband, sought reasons to justify his disappearance and appeared deeply distressed when she reflected on how he was managing to survive on his own without her. The therapist reflected back to Priathan the dramatic change in her view and wondered why she had apologised for her anger.

Priathan considered this for a few moments and said that it was the first time she had expressed such anger to another person about her husband. Priathan stated that she believed that it was inappropriate to express anger towards her husband as this might jeopardise the relationship, however she now feels that as she is not being judged, she found that she is able to voice the feelings that she had previously suppressed. The therapist invited Priathan to share how it had felt to be true to her feelings and to express them. Priathan said that although she doubted herself directly afterwards, she had felt courageous when she expressed the anger and continued to feel this now. The therapist then allowed Priathan to explore the validity of her felt experiences with the meaning that she attributed to them. Priathan reflected on her early childhood where as a young girl she was taught to be obedient in order to be good. Being an obedient girl also gained the approval of her parents and other community members, which made Priathan feel worthy. As a result, Priathan internalised that to get approval and be worthy she needed to be obedient to others. This helped her appreciate why she had prioritised everyone's needs above her own.

This insight also helped Priathan understand why she had been so frustrated with her children with their constant demands for attention. She realised that she had projected her anger onto her children rather than her abusers, whom she still felt powerless towards. She also blamed the host culture for allowing children to express themselves, which went against what she had been brought up to believe – that children were not allowed to have their own voice. Priathan began to understand and appreciate her children's need for self-expression, which she was not able to have in her childhood. This insight was empowering and Priathan began to gain self-esteem (Freud 1894).

Given the amount of cultural differences across communities and the fact that cultures are always evolving, the possibility of being competent in understanding different cultures, we suggest, is unrealistic. However, what is possible is having cultural humility that seeks to understand individuals from their own cultural frame of reference. Acknowledging our differences in the working relationship allows us to invite the client to share with us more about their culture and critically how they interpret it. We find Papadopoulos's analogy of a cloak instructive when considering such interpretations:

> a culture, if it means anything at all, should not be thought of as a kind of straightjacket, something tight and encompassing which limits movements… If any clothing analogy makes sense, it would be

> better to think of culture as a cloak, which could be worn in many ways, even taken off when not needed, or pulled tightly around the body when it's cold. It is a cloak of many patches: language, food habits, artistic traditions…moral rules…many of these features are adopted or manipulated by individuals, or, to keep the cloak analogy, sit lightly upon them and can be set aside at will. So, refugees are not 'prisoners' of their cultural differences, or ours. (Papadopolous 2002, p.75)

In subsequent sessions Priathan spoke of how her mother-in-law was repeatedly appearing in her nightmares. When she later learned of her death, Priathan was greatly distressed. She lived with the regret of leaving her mother-in-law behind, and her death meant that she was not present to perform the last cultural rituals of her burial, which would have been the case if she had not fled. Priathan attributed her nightmares, which at times included her mother-in-law's face watching her while she was being abused, to her failure of not being by her deathbed. The following session with the therapist was particularly telling.

Priathan said, 'I have been having disturbed sleep for months and this makes me very tired during the day.' When the therapist enquired about what Priathan understood by these dreams Priathan stated emphatically, 'My mother-in-law comes to visit me every time I try to sleep. She looks at me sadly and sometimes angrily.' The therapist paraphrased this using the word 'dreaming' to connect Priathan to reality and the present moment in which she was safe, and wondered why her mother-in-law was both sad and angry. Priathan explained, 'She is right to be angry. I did not look after her in her last days and I should have been by her bedside when she died. But how could I travel back home? It was dangerous. Yet she cannot rest in peace because of this and I feel terrible that I have let her down.' The therapist summarised, 'You believe you let your mother-in-law down by not being with her, yet can't see how you could have gone back to her safely.' Priathan concurred, 'That is right. I had to go back but I could not.'

With the therapist paraphrasing and summarising what Priathan had shared, Priathan began to connect more deeply within herself and became more congruent with her feelings. Having appreciated the cultural significance of the nightmares, and how these linked to her ancestors, the therapist sought cultural ways to make sense in resolving them. The therapist reaffirmed their cultural differences and asked Priathan how they resolved ancestral issues in her culture. Priathan responded, 'I first need to fast for ten days as a cleansing ceremony, then invite a few community members to a traditional prayer ceremony to honour and plead with my mother-in-law for forgiveness so she can rest in peace.'

While the therapist could offer other skills to help process Priathan's nightmares, she was aware that Priathan did not perceive her nightmare as an intra-psychic problem but as a supernatural belief. Through cultural humility, the therapist respected Priathan's way of resolving her concerns and embraced a resolution that was effective in resolving her distress, rather than attempting to interpret it as a nightmare which needed to be processed through revisiting traumatic events.

After a few weeks, Priathan reported, 'I have been sleeping much better since the cleansing ceremony. I am at peace with myself and believe that my mother-in-law has forgiven me.'

In this example, Priathan's cultural cloak fitted perfectly in resolving her issues around her mother-in-law and nightmares; whereas in the previous example her cultural cloak was very restrictive as she had introjected what she had been taught as a child, to be obedient and suppress her voice, and had become an adult who was unable to express herself.

From these examples, we hope practitioners will see the benefit of bearing witness and how it enables a refugee to process the loss, cultural conditioning and in some cases the trauma they have experienced. This can help reduce the psychological burden they have to carry, which in turn may make it easier for the practitioner to meet their needs.

Bearing witness to refugees requires practitioners to have psychological resilience in order to sit with the client's pain and allow them to articulate the full extent of their distress in order to empathise with their needs and find ways to meet them.

As we have seen with Priathan, her journey to exile involved traumatic events that were as bad as the ones she had experienced in her homeland and which had forced her to leave in the first place. To navigate these, she compromised her dignity in order to survive, which disrupted her self-identity to such an extent that interacting with other people became extremely difficult. For similar reasons, many refugees can feel very lonely and become isolated. However, it is also possible that refugees will respond to these traumatic events (or some of them) positively, with resilience, and even discover or develop strengths that enhance their self-identity (Papadopoulos 2007). So, while refugees often present in a psychologically distressed manner, it is essential to be aware that this is not the whole picture. The fact that they have survived to be talking to the practitioner at all is testimony to their inner resourcefulness, capability and resilience. The practitioner needs, therefore, to always hold in awareness the totality of the refugee's story, which is often a combination of trauma and triumph.

However, as the purpose of this book is to offer ways to work with refugees presenting with high levels of distress, our case studies represent clients who have experienced trauma. This can manifest in symptoms, such as post-traumatic stress disorder, which can cause a mental withdrawal from the recollection of their traumas so as not to be overwhelmed by them. As a result, the mind may experience gaps in memory concerning painful events or dates, as well as 'normal' times before these events that can be suppressed or even entirely forgotten. We suggest that the practitioner is aware of such conditions when bearing witness, as this can identify the impact of trauma on the refugee and whether they are coherent enough to engage within their service level or whether they need to be referred to a more specialist service.

Once identified as being within the remit of service, it is possible to offer psychoeducation that involves crisis intervention, normalising and mindfulness skills, and also translate their own cultural attitudes into mental health terminology in order to make sense of it.

LEARNING ACTIVITIES
Reflect on the scenarios below:

- When do you think it would be helpful for people to give you advice and when would you prefer them to simply listen to understand you?

- What is it like for you when a friend is in great distress and there was nothing practical you can offer?

- What is it like for you to support somebody who has different views and/or values from you?

CHAPTER 9

PSYCHOEDUCATION

A wise person knows there is something to be learned from everyone.

Anon

After reading this chapter and completing the learning activities provided, you should be able to:

• understand when a client will benefit from an intervention

• differentiate between practical and psychological interventions

• provide crisis intervention: normalising and mindfulness skills

• provide cultural sensitivity to mental health

• enable cultural re-adjustment

• provide practical orientation.

After bearing witness to the refugee's narrative and empathically understanding what is of the deepest concern to them, we need to identify, from our understanding of the refugee phenomena and the refugee's assessment, what practical and psychological information will be of value to them. We call this 'psychoeducation'. This is a combination of two elements: practical orientation which many refugees present with including casework and navigating the host country system and secondly, psychological therapies to respond to their emotional distress

Psychoeducation addresses the many and differing needs of refugees described in Part 1 of this book: crisis intervention, when clients are psychologically overwhelmed by traumatic events such as persecution described in Chapter 1, and loss or separation from loved ones in Chapter 2; cultural re-adjustment, to support host country acculturation, discussed in Chapter 3; practical orientation, to respond to the client's biopsychosocial needs through casework, as outlined in Chapter 4; and the cultural attitudes towards different understandings of the refugee mental health symptoms as explained in Chapter 6. Our hope is that all of these psychoeducational interventions will serve to empower self-identity and enhance resilience, as discussed in Chapter 5.

We have made psychoeducation our third principle because we know that different cultures have their own understandings of culture, beliefs, traditions and mental health symptoms. While it is essential to respect their views, if their distress and difficulty in engaging with services are as a result of their own interpretation or belief system, this could prevent them from meeting their needs. For this reason we offer psychoeducation interventions in a way that gives time and space to reflect on what benefit they may have by applying them.

In addition, many refugees come from countries in which their human rights have been abused through acts of oppression and by dictatorships, and have had to comply without question in order to survive. For women, if there is gender inequality, there may be an additional layer of abuse that has caused them to lack self-expression. If so, they may struggle to talk to the practitioner about their needs.

This means that the practitioner needs both to offer information and ensure that the manner in which they do so enables the refugee to question the validity it has for them.

Psychoeducation is a process of imparting useful information through therapeutic collaboration and wellbeing activities to help the refugee widen their choices by providing options previously unavailable to them, and normalising experiences that they may have not been aware of.

Psychoeducation in this case has two strands: Practical Orientation and Psychological Therapies.

Practical orientation

A person who relocates to a new country is faced by many administrative tasks and procedures that require lots of casework. For refugees, this starts with their basic needs of shelter, food, accommodation, legal support and health services. Providing them with useful information on how to address these ongoing issues would increase their understanding of their rights and responsibilities as well as reduce their distress and enhance their wellbeing. This information – imparted by the practitioner – is essential in allowing the refugee to make informed choices. For example, this could be sharing how one can access the health service or the procedure to see a dentist if this is what the client needs. Research carried out by Refugee Council in 2016 describes how challenging it is for newly recognised refugees to meet their psychosocial needs (Basedow and Doyle 2016).

For example, Priathan initially struggled to understand the information given to her. She found learning the host country language difficult, she found the transport system a challenge, she was scared to present her health needs to her doctor and also struggled with food shopping because she did not fully understand the information on the labels on jars, tins and packages.

'I feel like I am back in my first year, trying to learn how to walk again,' she reflected.

We have found that individually and cumulatively, psychoeducation is empowering and contributes to enhancing the wellbeing of the refugee.

Psychological therapies

A collaborative approach is taken in exploring options to expand the viewpoint of the refugee in their understanding of mental health symptoms and their possible causes, while introducing effective ways to manage or contain them. The practitioner and the client are encouraged to use different lenses to explore new possibilities, resulting in a different understanding of mental health symptoms, which may help to stabilise and regulate their feelings.

This is a sensitive intervention and one must be careful not to unravel the refugee's beliefs but to add another option or lens to view the presenting issues. This facilitates cross-cultural understanding where both interpretations are valid.

Crisis intervention: normalising and mindfulness skills

As we explained at the beginning of Chapter 7, the therapeutic relationship requires safety to be established from the start. This is also the foundation of Maslow's hierarchy of needs from which we provide information that starts with the priority of safety.

If the client is in mortal danger, it is important to immediately refer them to the emergency services. The issue could be biological, if they have a severe injury or illness; social, if in physical danger from others; and psychological, if they are suicidal or at risk of harming themselves. In such cases, appropriate referral to emergency services is essential to bring stability to the client as a priority before any further work can be done.

In cases where refugees are not in imminent mortal danger, but present in such psychological distress that they are unable to focus on anything in particular and struggle to talk, we suggest crisis intervention should be offered to them.

Crisis intervention includes putting experience into perspective, normalising feelings in relation to experiences, and offering information to help them make sense of their distress (see Appendix D). In addition, we can offer mindfulness skills. Kabat-Zinn (1994) defines mindfulness as: 'Paying attention in a particular way on purpose in the present moment, non-judgementally' (p.4). Felder, Dimidjian and Segal (2012) describe these as guided practices of sitting in awareness without talking, and noticing internal biological responses, commonly involving high levels of fear. For this reason, we offer practices that focus on the breath and scanning the body to help make the refugee feel safe and grounded. While we find that focusing on the breath can be a good place to start, if a refugee is very anxious this may draw attention to the discomfort of their breathing. In such cases, we offer simple ways to connect to the present moment, such as squeezing a stress ball or standing up straight with their back pressed against the surface of the wall.

This is a useful intervention when refugees present with overwhelming feelings of not being in control. For example, in the following situation with Priathan, we needed to offer crisis intervention in the fourth session.

For most of the session, Priathan looked extremely uncomfortable, as if she was holding something inside her that was desperate to come out. The therapist noticed this, so allowed her to choose when to open up by gently reflecting back Priathan's small talk in a way that demonstrated she was not going to push her to speak. Then, nearly halfway through the session, Priathan gave a deep breath and, as if allowing herself to contact this internal source of distress, gulped for air and blurted out: 'I feel I am going crazy.' She looked expectantly into the therapist's eyes, as if fearing what her reaction might be. Priathan continued, 'I don't think I can cope anymore. Every night I wake up sweating and my head is full of the most vivid images of what happened...' Her head dropped and her voice became almost inaudible: 'They tore my clothes.'

At this point the therapist stayed with and verbalised the palpable sense of fear in the room. Feeling heard, Priathan was able to disclose two things. First, how terrifying it was to keep remembering the time when she was raped by people in authority. Second, she revealed her fear that others would judge her as emotionally incapable of looking after her children and take them away. The therapist reflected that although this was hugely and understandably distressing, the flashbacks to the event of her traumatic experience were normal responses to an abnormal event. It was essential to allow space for bearing witness to explore and process feelings and experiences.

The therapist offered Priathan perspective on the fight/flight response – which causes the body to automatically react by running away, or staying to fight or freeze – as a natural evolutionary response to danger which her flashback to this terrifying event had triggered.

In doing so, Priathan was able to develop her agency and capacity to process the validity of the fight/flight response against her own experiences. In time, she was able to see that her feelings of rage, despair and depression that she formerly deemed unacceptable, were, in fact, normal, given her experience of powerlessness when she had been raped. As a result, she was able to start to develop a state of autonomy.

In addition to normalising her experience, the therapist also offered mindfulness skills to develop Priathan's capacity to reconnect with the present moment by focusing her attention through the five senses of sight, smell, touch, taste and sound. By focusing attention on the five senses one at a time, Priathan was able to connect to the present moment in which she was safe. That helped her to anchor herself to the reality of her current situation of safety when her flashbacks occurred that dragged her back to relive the terrifying ordeal of her past.

Normalising and mindfulness skills constitute two parts of what we term 'crisis intervention'. Normalising is a top-down intervention in which a cognitive explanation is made of the fight/flight response;

this includes offering an interpretation of symptoms as a natural response to lived experiences. This skill brings understanding rather than labelling symptoms or self-blame. Mindfulness skills, meanwhile, are bottom-up techniques that ground people in the present moment. This equips a person to become aware of the mind and its wandering state, and how one may learn the art of gently noticing what is going on within the body while bringing the mind back into the present and a safe environment. This allows the body to send messages to the brain to switch off the alarm activating the fight/flight response. As well as mindfulness skills, other types of self-help techniques can control traumatic symptoms. For example, cognitive-behavioural techniques, such as snapping an elastic band around the wrist when an individual starts to have intrusive thoughts, can serve to remind them that they can choose to not think about them.

Providing affirmation to Priathan was important. As we saw in Chapter 5, a person can present as vulnerable, but they also have strengths and resources. The practitioner reminded Priathan of these: how she had managed to escape with her two children and how, although it was difficult, she had managed to negotiate a risky journey to the host country. Her acknowledgement of this helped Priathan see herself in a different and more positive light.

Cultural re-adjustment

In the following session, Priathan presented in great distress: 'I don't know what has happened to my daughter,' she said. 'She has changed since we came to this country. She shouts at me and the other day even threw a glass of juice against the wall. I cannot go on like this. In my country we respect our parents, but she has no respect for me. When I try to speak to her she withdraws into herself and hides away in her room.'

The therapist asked if her daughter had always been like this. 'No, she never behaved like this before,' she reflected. 'This behaviour started three months after reaching this country.'

Although Priathan personally felt better after attending the previous session – by understanding her flashbacks she now felt more in control – she explained that the challenges of life in a very different culture were destabilising her. In Chapter 3 we saw the dilemma that Priathan faced when she was told that the physical punishment she had used to discipline her daughter in her home country was not acceptable in the host country. Priathan explained that she continued to struggle to find an alternative.

The therapist offered cultural re-adjustment to affirm that this type of punishment was indeed not acceptable, and to support Priathan to recognise the importance of finding alternatives, while also offering space for her to reflect on what this meant to her.

In doing so, Priathan was able to articulate how the importance of having respect for elders went unquestioned in her culture. She remembered that when she was a student she did not question her teachers and obeyed school rules. She also reflected that children 'were to be seen but not heard' and that bad behaviour was met with physical punishment. The therapist empathised with her experiences and wondered how she had coped. Bowlby's (1952) hypothesis that parents' ability to care for their children is based on the parenting they received themselves could contribute to understanding why Priathan was always on her best behaviour, constantly prioritising the needs of others in order to please them.

The therapist observed that Priathan's early conditions of worth had an impact on her capacity to parent her daughter within the expected culture, but she also commended Priathan's willingness to find better ways to communicate with her daughter about sensitive information.

In addition, although the daughter was not the therapist's client, she held in awareness the possibility that Priathan's daughter was acting out this extreme behaviour in order to express thoughts or feelings she might otherwise be incapable of articulating. For this reason, the therapist recommended that they attend family therapy to help them rebuild their relationship and address any underlying issues.

The therapist also booked Priathan into a psychoeducation workshop on boundaries and assertiveness to help her identify her psychological needs and learn new ways to manage her personal space, which would also support her in managing her daughter's behaviour.

In the tenth session, Priathan explained that her relationship with her daughter had improved after she had been to the counselling session advised by the doctor. Priathan was also attending a refugee women's group and, during a parenting workshop, was surprised to find a number of women were experiencing similar challenges with their adolescent children. It was comforting for her to know that she was not alone and that she was not incapable of parenting but, rather, that she needed to understand the development stages her daughter was going through. The group was empowering and Priathan learned interventions that were effective to support her daughter and also improve their relationship.

'I can now see that I had not given my daughter space to share what all this experience meant to her,' said Priathan. 'I had assumed that because I gave her food and essentials that was enough, but it didn't seem to be. So I was afraid that she might need something I was not able to provide.'

Cultural attitudes to mental health

Many of us have different understandings of mental health symptoms. For some refugees, their interpretation of these symptoms can differ widely from the host country perspective. This could present a challenge when it comes to diagnosing the psychological needs of some refugees. In some cultures, mental health symptoms have a social stigma that hinders people from accessing mental health services. Other cultures attribute these symptoms to evil spirits and other traditional beliefs. Many of these cultures present mental health as somatic complaints which may lead to inappropriate diagnosis.

Offering a different perspective on understanding mental health symptoms empowers the client to decide on any appropriate change from which they might benefit. It also offers an opportunity to discuss this change, and if it would give them the improved wellbeing outcome they desire. It is important to recognise at this point that change involves risks and losses. In Priathan's case, although she may gain from being empowered, she might also experience a loss of her cultural belief and values she has held since childhood – and this could impact on her self-concept. It's therefore essential to fully explore these changes with the refugee so that they understand the risks involved, and how best to implement, manage and commit to them, and sustain them.

Having built sufficient trust in her therapist, Priathan was able to talk in depth about her shame and reflect on her cultural conditioning and all the assumptions she previously believed were fact. She was also able to identify the cultural cognitive thinking she accessed when her therapist reflected her expression that she had always had a painful life. She said she had not always followed the life of a spiritual woman as expected in her culture. Priathan believed that the suffering she was now experiencing was a result of her shameful acts and uncleanliness from her past experiences, and that this justified her suffering. She also believed that she had played a part in the acts and blamed herself profoundly.

Through psychoeducation, Priathan was able to appreciate that her physical symptoms and feelings of self-blame, guilt and shame may have been a result of her being – in her words – a 'bad person'. This negative interpretation then triggered overwhelming emotions and unhealthy physical reactions, which were all a product of her negative thinking.

Priathan's belief system played a significant part in her distress and psychological pain. Although she recognised that she was helpless and had no choice in most cases, she did, however, reproach herself, thinking she was 'guilty' and deserved to 'suffer for her abuse'. Through psychoeducation, issues are externalised and addressed from different perspectives, and this enabled Priathan to share and learn about different perspectives on mental health symptoms and allowed her to widen her understanding. In turn, this enabled her to be more informed in making choices that increased her feelings of optimism and encouragement with regard to her faith.

While the practitioner must remain congruent, it is essential they develop a compassionate approach to introducing sensitive views in a way that is not confrontational to an individual's belief system.

As a consequence of these psychoeducational interventions, Priathan stated that she felt more reassured and hopeful about her transforming self-identity. In addition, the resources she had gained – of cultural re-adjustment and practical orientation via the therapeutic alliance – increased her resilience to cope with the ongoing challenges of the asylum process.

Having illustrated practical and psychological psychoeducation through work with Priathan, we will now provide an overview of psychoeducation in the context of Maslow's hierarchy of needs.

Providing psychoeducation where it is needed

As we have seen with Priathan, asylum-seeking and refugee people present with multiple levels of needs. For this reason, having a clear structure from which to meet these needs is, in our view, of great value. We believe that Maslow's hierarchy of needs is such a structure because it offers a clear sequence to follow, with opportunities for psychoeducational interventions to be given throughout. It starts with basic needs that, once met, enable higher needs to be addressed.

We will now apply this hierarchy to a recently arrived asylum seeker who has made an extremely challenging journey, often risking life and limb en route. First, they will have physiological needs of food and water and may need medical intervention due to dehydration, injury and illness. This leads into the second level of safety: the physical integrity of the body. In such cases, ensuring clients know how to access medical services is the top priority. The next priority – if their physical health is good or being tended to – is housing. They need a safe place to live, and enough money to buy necessities or gain access to food and clothing.

For asylum-seeking people, safety is sought not only in the physical structure of a house but, more widely, in the country as a whole. When they are granted refugee status, the country becomes a home, their new homeland. This also relates to Maslow's third hierarchy of belonging, in which the social bonds of family and friends create a personal home within the country. Psychoeducation that meets the need for belonging is initially practical orientation: for example, finding a solicitor who can present their asylum case, which, if successful, will allow them to have a new home in the host country. However, while they may belong in a legal sense – by being entitled to a passport and granted free access to the country – they may still feel out of place. This could detrimentally effect their need for self-esteem. This should not be a surprise: they have been uprooted from their home country (one they knew and could function in) and are starting again in a new land where they may feel out of place. Specifically, this could be because they are not understood as an individual (for example, by not speaking English) or, more generally, because they feel culturally alienated, especially if they have been brought up in a very different tradition to that of the host country.

If this is the case, psychoeducation around cultural adjustment can be key. At a fundamental level, education about the laws of the host country may be crucial to ensure they will respect these – and so be respected by its people in return. As we have seen in Priathan's home culture, the disciplining of children with physical punishment is seen as necessary for instilling the child's respect in that country's laws and institutions. However, in host countries where physically punishing children is a crime, parents who do so risk being both imprisoned and having their children removed from them and put into care.

For the refugee, this presents internal conflicts and feelings of helplessness and overload on many levels. Psychoeducation is therefore essential in order to explain the host country's attitudes and values so the refugee can establish a certain level of fundamental competence in their new environment.

Other factors that help to build self-esteem are achievement and confidence. For many, this is a feeling that comes with a chosen career. However, in host countries where asylum seekers are forbidden to work, or where highly qualified professionals can work but are unable to practice due to a lack of recognition of qualification and language barrier (and so are forced to take jobs not requiring verbal communication, such as labouring), their self-esteem could be compromised. In such cases, psychoeducation about volunteering in organisations and courses in the host country language, for example, can be a valuable way for them to regain their self-esteem.

Throughout these four levels of need – physiological, safety, belonging and esteem – psychoeducation seeks to give the asylum-seeking person the chance to become an equal in the host country. This is achieved by accessing the same rights to health, housing, refugee status and life purpose – by having a doctor, a place to live, a solicitor and work (or by volunteering in organisations if paid employment is forbidden) respectively.

Traumatic experiences are associated with depressive symptoms such as low mood, distress, despair and hopelessness. These impact on one's ability to function at an individual and family level and can cause disruption in relationships.

Priathan's psychoeducation sessions included challenging her belief system, myths, unhealthy practices in her diet, and her reliance on medication to relieve stress. The work was also focused on enhancing her communication skills, building a support network and coping skills, positive thinking, social skills, stress management and expanded social support. Afterwards she reported a reduction in low moods, increased self-esteem and an improvement in self-advocacy skills, all of which helped her avoid further victimisation.

In learning some grounding techniques and improving her nutrition, Priathan was able to reconnect her self-esteem to her body image, resulting in enhanced self-esteem and self-acceptance. She also gained improved strategies relating to parenting skills, widened her social support, and enhanced her cognitive-behavioural techniques and methods for relaxation.

Priathan's daughter also improved as she started to recognise her negative social behaviour and wanted to replace it with more constructive and affirmative responses and actions.

Priathan's relationship with her daughter improved as they both began to feel compassion towards each other's experiences, creating a space in which love and affection for each other could develop.

While this book focuses on working in a one-to-one relationship between a practitioner and a refugee client, in Part 3, in Chapter 10, we focus on group work that promotes community engagement because we have witnessed how refugees flourish within such a group setting that offers the experience of a familiar extended family. We are also aware of many goodwill community sponsorship programmes that make a positive difference in refugees' lives and which may benefit from extra tools for effective therapeutic interventions, to which we hope this will be a contribution.

The refugee phenomenon would also not be complete without the understanding of the impact that conflict and violence have on separated asylum-seeking children and how we might shape our services to work with them more effectively, which we cover in Chapter 11.

LEARNING ACTIVITIES
Reflect on something you learned that enabled you to have a different perspective.

- Where did your previous understanding come from and what influenced you to change your views?

- What have you learnt from a culture very different from your own that has caused you to question your own?

- What is it like for you to be in a foreign country without understanding the system?

▓ PART 3 ▓

WORKING WITH GROUPS AND SEPARATED CHILDREN

Part 3 of this book is divided into two chapters:

Chapter 10: Building on Strengths and Resilience through Community Engagement. Rebuilding collective cultures to promote wellbeing and enhance integration.

Chapter 11: Working with Separated Children Asylum Seekers. Effective ways of working with unaccompanied asylum-seeking children in meeting their psychosocial needs.

While this book focuses on working in a one-to-one relationship between a practitioner and a refugee client, in Part 3 we focus on group work in Chapter 10 that promotes community engagement because we have witnessed how refugees flourish within such a group setting that offers the experience of a familiar extended family. We are also aware of many goodwill community sponsorship programmes that make a positive difference in refugees' lives, and may benefit from extra tools for effective therapeutic interventions which we hope this will be a contribution to.

The refugee phenomenon would also not be complete without the understanding of the impact that conflict and violence have on separated asylum seeking children and how we might shape our services to work with them more effectively which we cover in Chapter 11.

CHAPTER 10

BUILDING ON STRENGTHS AND RESILIENCE THROUGH COMMUNITY ENGAGEMENT

The restoration of social bonds begins with the discovery that one is not alone. Nowhere is this experience more immediate, powerful, or convincing than in a group... The solidarity of a group provides the strongest protection against terror and despair, and the strongest antidote to traumatic experience. Trauma isolates; the group re-creates a sense of belonging.

Judith L Herman (1992)

After reading this chapter and completing the learning activities provided you should be able to:

- understand the benefits of building community activities – these include reducing social isolation, creating a sense of belonging and allowing refugees to express their voice

- empower through normalising experiences and shared learning

- understand how to develop your interpersonal skills that enhance wellbeing through community engagement

- promote awareness and harness local resources to provide a sense of home to refugees

- appreciate how an open and inclusive society can promote integration in local communities.

This section is for those compassionate members of the community from different disciplines, including religious, cultural or social activity groups, who are so willing to participate in this field. We believe that having an awareness of the value of a community is essential. This is because all refugees have lost the community of their homeland and many come from a collective culture in which life is experienced and decisions are made together. Encouraging refugees in the host country to recreate communities facilitates a space in which traditions, cultures and belief systems can be shared and expressed with equality. In such an environment, group members enhance their coping mechanisms, reduce social isolation and promote wellbeing. They feel safe to use a narrative approach in order to recount their life experiences in relation to their current circumstances, and this enables them to identify and tap into their resilience and develop their potential.

Working together to identify needs and find solutions

As we have previously discussed, while refugees have gone through traumatic experiences, including violence, conflict and displacement, this does not necessarily mean that they are traumatised and present with pathological symptoms.

The fact that they are survivors of conflict and violence informs us that they have innate capacities and personal resources which, given the appropriate support, they can access once again.

In order to facilitate such interpersonal growth, we are mindful that while most Western approaches encourage individual autonomy, for many refugees a collective approach that focuses on the 'self in relation to others' can bring valuable meaning and structure to their lives. This means that while we provide them with necessary individual support, it is highly beneficial also to facilitate a connection for them to participate in community activities. This allows them to recreate networks that provide a platform to express lived experiences that can be shared and understood within a collective context. We have found that there is immense healing and empowerment that comes with sharing experiences and learning from each other through psychosocial group settings. This is not surprising given that many refugees come from such a collective culture in which celebrations and grieving are experienced within a community context.

However, as well as this common shared experience (that is likely to be welcomed) as refugees by definition have been persecuted in their homeland from which they have been exiled, there can also be a fear of engaging in a group. This was the case for Priathan in the host country when she took almost a year to agree to a referral by her social worker to attend a psychosocial women's group to enhance her self-esteem. At first Priathan was reluctant to attend, but her social worker encouraged her and she chose to go to see how it would be.

After attending four sessions, Priathan was surprised to find how many of the other women in the group seemed to share similar experiences to her. She had initially been paranoid, thinking that they knew about her and had made negative judgements towards her, but later suddenly had a realisation that they genuinely held nothing against her. In that moment Priathan became tearful and for the first time experienced a profound sense of belonging. She felt safe and this enabled her to find her voice and express her experience. As the other women sat in silence, Priathan felt the warmth of acceptance as she shared for the first time in the group.

'This group has taught me how to be brave and courageous to share experience in the group. One woman spoke in a caring manner and also saw the courageous side of how I dealt with my traumatic experience. This made me feel reassured and I felt like a survivor for the first time. I felt alive. This group became my family, a sisterhood. We all listened to each other with such compassion and care, but most of all I learned that the abuse was not my fault and I should not blame myself.'

As this example shows, as well as meeting the social needs for belonging, a group can also provide ways of meeting fundamental needs of personal sustenance and safety within which psychological needs of self-esteem and self-actualisation can flourish (Maslow 1943).

Such community engagement offers refugees the possibility to be human and to feel united by focusing on a common task. This non-directive approach means that there is no stigma attached to any member, as each is completely accepted and valued by the others in the group. In this environment, each member contributes their skills and internal resources and is appreciated through their unique response to the activity rather than according to their definition as an individual presenting with psychological difficulties. Through such groups, refugees develop a sense of belonging, perceiving themselves as a collective, which for many is a more comfortable and familiar way of relating to self within their cultural context.

Group participation offers opportunities for externalising issues and learning coping skills. Psychologically, the group provides an empowering context for its members to not only cope, by reducing distress and improving wellbeing, but also to develop, by discovering new possibilities. As with Priathan, the learning comes from the examples of how some group members successfully addressed problems that others previously experienced as intractable.

While there are different ways in which these levels of psychological wellbeing can be achieved, the following points illustrate some of the valuable benefits we have found in the many groups we facilitate:

- Group members' distress tends to reduce when bearing witness to each other's hitherto 'frozen' traumatic experiences that, once released, can allow both individual and collective healing processes to begin. Mindfulness and compassion to self are shared and practised by the group and this enhances their resilience, resulting in increased self-esteem.

- The wellbeing of individuals in the group, who behave destructively alone, often increases when they collectively agree a standard of behaviour (social norms) that replaces their previously harmful neurotic reactions, often acted out from anger and frustration. With helpful and considered responses they can articulate their needs and invite others to contribute to them.

- Psychological development can occur when people hear accounts of how others triumphed in adversity, whereby new strengths developed have been commensurate to the magnitude of the challenge they faced. These narratives become a wellspring of inspiration from which others in the group can draw, and new possibilities for action emerge by applying the principles of what worked.

In these ways, groups enable refugees to be a resource for each other. Members can learn how the same traumatic event can produce very different psychological outcomes by virtue of the way it is cognitively framed (with acceptance or judgement) and the manner by which it is responded to (with curiosity or blame).

As needs are of such importance we are always seeking resources to support this in our work. We have found Kinyon and Lasater's (2015) exposition of three meta-categories of universal need – wellbeing, connection and self-expression – helpful in informing how we can provide for the needs of our clients.

While wellbeing can be developed alone (for example, through meditation and physical exercise) and connection requires others to socially engage with, the need for self-expression can be met both alone (such as by writing and painting) and with others (for example, by performing music or drama).

We will now consider the benefits of each in a refugee context, starting with connection, then wellbeing and, finally, self-expression, using examples from the groups we facilitate and how we tailor them to suit our clients' needs.

Our clients express that they frequently feel lonely in a country with unfamiliar cultural practices and where a different language is spoken, and that belonging to a group reduces their isolation. For such clients, a group that offers a space in which they can share their experiences and concerns is greatly appreciated.

However, many refugees fear that other group members may disclose what they have said to those outside who seek to persecute them. For this reason, groups can be provided to offer activities that do not require their narrative to be told. These groups can be presented to such clients as being able to meet needs for both their wellbeing and self-expression, which also, by virtue of being located with others, will automatically meet their need for connection.

Wellbeing can be developed in a group that focuses on a particular subject, such as mindfulness skills, which the individual can practise alone, for example through mindful breathing and exercises such as the body scan. This can also meet their need for connection, by practising together each session and enjoying conversations about the subject they are learning that do not require disclosure of their confidential narrative.

Similarly, the need for self-expression can be met in groups offering resources for creativity, such as jewellery making. This allows refugees to connect by physically sharing the space with others while also being able to work alone, absorbed in their creation. We have found that a particular benefit of such settings in which words are not needed is that there is space to talk, though no obligation to do so.

This gives refugees who do want to express their concerns, but would be too intimidated to be in a group whose sole purpose is to do so, an opportunity to broach these in their own time.

Self-expression in a group can also be totally collaborative, for example drama therapy requires each member to perform a role for the piece to work. For refugees who have lost their role, whether personally, as a family member or professionally, without their career, this provides a way to reconnect to these traditions and structures of self-expression. They can be recreated by asking other members of the group to represent the family they lost and colleagues they no longer have.

From offering such groups we have learned that the need for self-expression is particularly valuable in a refugee context of persecution. This is because self-expression is often suppressed, for example when a country is colonised and the language of the occupier or oppressor quite literally replaces the mother tongue (Memmi 1957). A group offers a way for refugees suppressed in such ways to recover their voice, their original language, by using it to talk to others (Martín-Baró 1964). In addition, as a consequence of being in another country with different customs and practices, a refugee has an opportunity to assess whether the cultural conditioning of their homeland that deems them to *have to be* – what Rogers (1959) describes as 'conditions of worth'– matches the self-expression of *who they really are*. Through this process, it may then become possible to live more authentically, in a way of their choosing. Refugees may also find aspects of the host country incongruent and by challenging these bring change to the country as a whole or create what they need by forming a community within it.

The key learning in a group involves:

- the development of positive relationships through group activity interactions

- sharing and learning healthy coping skills

- mindfulness skills that increase self-compassion

- proactivity in meeting group goals, hence promoting self-esteem

- a realistic attitude to change, including the loss of home, through group feedback.

Each of these points can be a small step to enhance resilience in clients as they support each other both emotionally and through their interpersonal skills.

However, in addition to loss and persecution in their homeland, refugees also face present challenges in the host country (Kunz 1973).

Promoting awareness and harnessing local resources to provide communities for refugees

Some challenges that refugees face are triggered by the wider social political discourse in the current host country regarding refugees. Some community members lack the awareness or understanding of what a refugee or asylum seeker's rights and entitlements are and this creates room for incorrect information or half-truths to develop, which could overspill into stereotypes and create prejudice in some communities. There are also many community members who empathise with the plight of refugees but lack the information or knowledge about how best to support them. For this reason, there is need for ongoing work to improve community awareness, where refugees are embraced as human beings first and foremost, and to create communities that are all-inclusive and accepting of a diverse cultural membership. In addition, having a community-led approach helps to nurture the resources that refugees bring to the host country as they experience a sense of belonging.

As we previously highlighted through the use of the Trauma Grid, many refugees come with strengths and innate capabilities that if nurtured well they would be able to re-connect with their skills including previous professional careers and flourish again.

The following two accounts demonstrate building resilience through engagement in a community programme.

The case of Arufat demonstrates this when he was referred to a refugee health professional programme to help him reclaim his medical career. At first he could not see this as a possibility. He had started looking for manual labour jobs, which did not require language skills, and he had dismissed the idea of being capable of learning the host country language and then retraining in a foreign language as a doctor.

'I am now 47 years old. I have gone through so much already and I miss my family a lot. I cannot see how I could fully learn a new language let alone requalify as a doctor in that new language.'

Arufat felt frustrated at having to start again and prove himself, having achieved the requisite qualifications in his homeland. He had many years of experience treating various medical ailments which included carrying out operations yet he felt he would not be deemed good enough due to the requirement in the host country to requalify. In addition, to do this in another language he had yet to learn appeared to him to be an insurmountable barrier.

After a year attending language classes and talking through his distress in therapeutic counselling, Arufat was encouraged to go to an induction session to assess whether he felt he now could succeed, with an option to opt out if he found it too great a task. Arufat attended the next programme in which he was part of a group of six other doctors from different countries. During their introductions, Arufat heard a range of experiences about starting the programme. A few people expressed great anxiety, others were sceptical but curious to find out more. Some said that they were fully determined to succeed, stating with great determination that what they had already survived and overcome was much greater than this and, therefore, believed that through the support of the programme they would succeed in reclaiming their professional status. A group member was moved to get up and ask everyone there to start referring to each other as doctors, regardless of whether they were practising or not. Another said that he would not allow his persecutors to win by taking away his hard-earned knowledge and so had determined to take this programme to defeat them! The whole group clapped for them and the increased resilience in the room, the will and motivation to conquer, was palpable.

As Arufut said, 'I was so shocked and surprised that what was shared resonated in me and what I had been going through in isolation due to fear and feelings of inadequacy, which now I realise was the aim of my abusers. Although it was early days in the programme and I still had my self-doubt, I also felt compelled to be in unity with my group and this meeting was the turning point of having an open mind to explore possibilities of reclaiming parts of me that I thought were no longer available.'

The programme created a community environment where all members of the group relied on and supported each other, discussed challenges and found possible solutions. In doing so the group developed certain values and norms which became part of their community culture.

'We took on the task as a group first to encourage each other in improving in the host country language,' Arufut commented. 'We decided that we would communicate only in the one language while in the group. We also thoroughly refreshed our medical knowledge and skills before taking any exams. We built such a resilient peer group support network it gave me a sense of belonging and completely changed my perception from "impossible" to "yes I can" and this became my mantra.'

The group members, however, were very grateful to the programme facilitators. Although they were not from a medical background, they had therapeutic skills and an ability to bear witness when individuals felt down or discouraged by the system and when group members faced prejudice while on placement. The programme facilitators were always keen to listen and empathise with group members' struggles in an encouraging and supportive way.

The programme facilitators adapted a multidisciplinary approach where they created various working relationships with other agencies. This meant they could refer the group members on where different needs were involved, and hence had a well-structured, co-ordinated, holistic response to their clients' needs.

Recreating communities is therefore an important and effective therapeutic intervention for refugee people as it constructs a sense of 'home' through their collective membership.

The other benefit of community engagement is the harnessing of the wealth of cultural resources which can contribute richly to their psychosocial wellbeing where challenges are addressed as a collective rather than on an individual basis.

Bion (1961) described how groups generated emotional culture to respond to anxiety and uncertainty which could be a conscious or unconscious way to be in control and avoid fear, anxiety or threat to their self-esteem. Furthermore, Menzies (1989) referred to a socially structured defence mechanism against anxiety which relies on the idea of splitting as a social defence.

Another community engagement programme was based on a women's group setting, which Priathan attended on a weekly basis.

The group initially started as a jewellery-making group using different types of beads. Priathan found this group valuable as it connected her to a community and she was not expected to share her sad stories. Initially she was quiet and too shy to speak, lacking confidence in her voice. However, over time more women shared their distress in the group and the rest were all there to support each other when one was down. The group facilitator provided a no-agenda open group process and allowed the group to take its organic formation.

Priathan felt connected by just being a member of the group where she was able to express herself through creative work. This group represented her family setting back home and she started to draw strength and enhance her resilience from this community setting.

'One of the powerful activities we did as a group was the Tree of Life programme,' she said. 'It was so enjoyable and yet very powerful. I discovered my strengths through that activity and together we made a strong bond to weather any storms in life.'

Priathan was not conversant in speaking or writing using the host country language and this was a barrier to her communication. However, the facilitator, with the help of an interpreter, encouraged her to draw a tree in stages, which represented her. At the start, she did not connect with this symbolism but the facilitator was very gentle and empathic in explaining the stages and Priathan found that she was able to communicate through drawing her cultural mango tree.

In week one the group members drew the first stage of the tree (roots) which they used to rewrite their life stories not as victims but as the authors to their narrative.

Priathan reflected on week one, 'I enjoyed drawing my mango tree, which was standing at the bottom of our garden in my country. This represented my family, cultural food, traditional celebrations like dancing and singing. I feel proud that I come from a rich culture with good values and norms. This group is my anchor now, where I can begin to flourish again.'

In week two, the group members drew the ground, which represented the here and now, and they were able to share their current lifestyle and any challenges they were going through. This created thinking on how they could get together to advocate for social issues they found unfair or discriminating. This collective decision enhanced the group resilience.

In week three, the group members drew the trunk of the tree. Priathan's mango tree was strong and solid, which is what she had unconsciously related to. Discussing the trunk enabled Priathan to draw strength from her mango tree and recognise her resilience through her interpersonal skills and caring for other people, as she was always willing to help and listen. She could see that she used these skills to look after her family back home but had taken her character for granted. This was very reassuring and affirming to her self-concept.

In week four, the group members drew the branches of the tree. Priathan struggled to engage with the discussions, as branches represented hopes, dreams and wishes for the future. She found it difficult to get beyond the fact that she had not been granted refugee status and was still in fear of being removed to the country where she had experienced persecution. However, there were others in the group with similar status and together they externalised the fear, making it more manageable to express and process in a contained manner. The group decided to hypothesise and share what their life would look like in future if all went well and they were granted safety. This was something to look forward to.

In week five, the group members drew leaves, which represented significant people in their lives, alive or dead.

'I am not sure I will give my husband a leaf,' Priathan said initially. 'I am in this situation because of his activities. My parents and my mother-in-law are very important to me as they taught me a lot about how to be a respectable woman.'

After group discussions, Priathan agreed that her husband deserved a leaf as he had played a significant part in her life; she also decided to forgive him and make peace within herself, getting rid of any feelings of resentment she harboured towards him.

In week eight, the group members drew fruits. This represented sharing with others through the art of giving and receiving either gifts or in kindness to one another. The group decided to make each other a bead necklace and to hold regular monthly meetings where they could stay connected and support each other in life through a sisterhood group.

> 'The last week was so powerful. We stood together and displayed our colourful trees with fruits. We created a strong forest which could stand all kinds of weather! This message was very strong and made us realise that as a community we are strong and resilient. Although some branches looked weak and two members did not complete the task, their trunk stood within our forest and this meant that they too were survivors and strong.'
>
> Ncazelo Ncube (REPSSI) and David Denborough
> (Dulwich Centre Foundation)
> http://dulwichcentre.com.au/the-tree-of-life

Conclusion

Refugee community organisations, local community groups and religious settings have played a significant part in encouraging a wider community engagement and being resourceful in building resilience and enhancing integration. These groups offer refugees a platform of self-expression from a collective culture which is more familiar and empowering.

We hope the possibilities we have witnessed in our groups for meeting the needs of wellbeing, connection and self-expression will become accessible for all refugees given that many come from collective cultures in which individual activities such as one-to-one counselling are not understood.

LEARNING ACTIVITIES

Reflect on a time you have been part of a group:

- Were there times you felt you found your voice and were there times you felt it hard to speak?

- What did the group dynamic tell you about your character?

- What did being part of this group mean to you?

CHAPTER 11

WORKING WITH SEPARATED CHILDREN ASYLUM SEEKERS

You have to understand, no one puts their children in a boat unless the water is safer than the land.

Warsan Shire

Although they share some of the same traumatic background as adult refugees, separated asylum-seeking children arrive in the host country with a whole group of very specific psychological and social issues.

When people are faced with conflict, human rights abuse or other social and political factors, sometimes the only way to keep safe is to flee. Despairing of their futures, families go through the Homeland Phase of Apprehension, anxiously trying to find ways to protect themselves and their loved ones from the dangers they face. However, as the conflicts escalate, families may have to decide what they can do to save themselves. For those with limited resources, this could simply mean abandoning their homes and setting off by foot towards the nearest border or refugee camp.

One must bear in mind that refugee children are often sent away out of love and the need to protect them. Sometimes, families feel they have no choice but to make the heart-rending decision to separate the family, staying behind while sending their children away on their own to safety. This can be because escaping from an oppressive government or a war-torn country can be very expensive and saving the children can use up all of a family's resources. In other circumstances, parents may decide they need to stay behind to look after elderly relatives, or to try to keep hold of their homes. In many cases, families become separated on the journey, with the children forced to find their own way to safety alone. Some may have been trafficked – forced into sexual or commercial exploitation, or sometimes into domestic servitude.

The journey to exile can be rough, and separated children are exceptionally vulnerable, facing huge risks along the way. They may have to travel through several countries, with no legal help, and no one to turn to for protection. The people with them may have no concern for their safety as children. It can take months to reach safety, with the children forced to walk day and night, in dangerous and physically draining conditions. Most will go hungry and the risks of physical injury and sickness are high. Some may become victims of physical or sexual abuse. Many lone child refugees find themselves being forced into child slavery in countries along the way, or thrown into illegal detention camps. Even when they may have made the land journey in relative safety, many will find themselves aboard dangerous and overcrowded boats, travelling at night with no lights and no life-saving equipment. They may suffer the trauma of capsizing, and having to watch their loved ones drown in front of them.

Once they arrive in the host country, they can feel overwhelmed by an accumulation of difficult feelings around their sense of loss and separation. This can trigger ambivalent feelings of not wanting to stay and at the same time being fearful of going back to their country. They may have a sense of both hope and anxiety over the uncertainty of the future (Papadopoulos 2002). Most separated children will arrive in the host country assuming that the worst is now over for them. The realisation that they may be caught up in layers of legality around their asylum claim, and that there is no guarantee that they will be allowed to remain, can lead to overwhelming levels of anxiety and feelings of rejection by the very people they had believed would offer them a safe future.

Asylum-seeking children are caught up in an unstable and uncertain phase based on heightened fear and the traumatic after-effects of the loss of loved ones and everything they have ever known. These experiences can delay or disrupt the natural pace of developmental stages all children go through from birth to their transition to adulthood (Erikson 1968). Depending on their psychological, physical and social circumstances, these are factors that might impact on how they engage with the host country and the children's capacity to integrate into local communities.

Practical

Accommodation
Legal support
Health services
Subsistence
Clothing
Family contacts
Language barrier
Education

Psychological

Loss and separation
Grief
Traumatic events
Discrimination
Social isolation
Impact on self-esteem
Culture shock
Uncertainty
Fear

Figure 11.1: Multiple levels of needs of separated asylum-seeking children

We have drawn on Harris's work (1998) that suggest how the environment and especially the peer group has a significant influence in shaping the development of the child's attitude, beliefs, knowledge, and skills within the culture they are grow up. Harris further acknowledges that although parents play a significant role in influencing the child, this is however only one part of the child's development. This is particularly salient for refugee children who in most cases develop within a collective culture and hence their personality is influenced by the community they interact with and their need to fit in.While every child is unique and will respond differently to adversity, all will have been separated from their families and friends and lost their home. Practitioners are encouraged to work creatively, often non-verbally, always allowing the child to direct the pace and direction of their therapy, and often using culturally sensitive therapies involving play, narrative, art, drama and movement. Furthermore, Melzak (2009) suggested working creatively using different modalities that respond to psychosocial needs as an effective approach in working with children.

The refugee child may also feel they are being beset with questions and information-gathering by all the different officials concerned with their care. They are frequently expected to attend multidisciplinary meetings and to fill in form after form. We recognise that many of these children may never have had experience of outside agencies being concerned with, and having authority over, their social welfare. This can be very confusing and sometimes, particularly where they are being questioned about their past, can even be re-traumatising. They may also experience these agencies as punishing or hostile, such as when the child's age is being disputed, or when they find themselves being moved to different areas or foster placements against their wishes.

To establish a therapeutic relationship, it is essential to offer a safe and nurturing space where children can find some peace and quiet if they want it. Questions should be kept to a minimum, and be asked at the initial assessment and when we are explaining what we can offer. It is important to always ask how they are feeling to gauge their mental wellbeing and avoid interrogating them or expecting them to share their story when they are not willing to do so. In other words, refugee children just need our non-conditional presence in order to feel safe.

We bear witness to whatever they tell us and listen empathically. It's all about finding some peace from the internal chatter and external pressure. We might sit on the carpet, throwing a ball backwards and forwards, look at pictures, draw things or do warm-up exercises to relax the body. Later we might explore issues like sleep disturbances, providing them with useful information about why they're having trouble at night and putting it in a context that lets them know they're not alone in this. When we are working with them, the child knows they can come every week for 12 weeks, and this gives them some clear boundaries, and models continuity and consistency of support in a world full of uncertainty and changes.

We recognise that every case is unique and the case study below does not suggest that one size fits all; however, we believe there is some learning we can share through it.

KRISHANTI

Krishanti is one of five siblings; he was the third born and the only boy in the family. His parents were active community members and they were a close-knit family. They prayed and ate together every evening. Krishanti was a popular boy at school and did well in his exams. His father was well respected in the community and loving to his family, although he was fairly strict and expected all his children to obey him. When civil war broke out and his father feared Krishanti would be forced to join the army, he paid a local man to get his son out of the country to safety. Krishanti had no choice in the matter and said his tearful goodbyes. He recalled that from that moment on, he lived with the constant fear of losing his family.

The journey to the host country took three months. Krishanti was one of several refugees, including some boys of a similar age, whose families had paid the people smugglers to get them to safety. They travelled at night so they would not be seen by patrols, risking their lives navigating the dangerous mountain paths with no torches. During the day, the boys would eat their food together and try to grab some sleep, always listening out for danger. They made their way through several countries.

When Krishanti's money ran out the people smugglers threw him out of the group, abandoning him in a strange country. He met another refugee who helped him find his way to a refugee camp. Every morning he would follow the other refugees trying to sneak onto a lorry going to another country, getting badly beaten by the local people smugglers because he could not pay them. Eventually he succeeded in getting there. As soon as he arrived he was directed to the immigration office to claim asylum. He was immediately asked his age. As he had never celebrated a birthday in his country, the social worker helped him work out an estimated age based on his physical appearance and what he had told her about his life at home.

It is notable that the process of assessing age to determine if someone is a child can be frightening as the consequences of an incorrect assessment may result in the child being denied their needs and subjected to detention along with adults (Dennis 2012).

In Krishanti's case, the social worker put his age as 15 and he was therefore entitled to care under the Children Act 1989. His first placement with a foster family broke down after three months because the family circumstances changed and they were no longer able to look after a child. Although the social worker explained this was not his fault, Krishanti started to feel a sense of rejection, unconsciously mirroring the loss of his family. He felt unwanted and that the world was not to be trusted.

In his second placement, his foster mother was very kind and understanding, but by now, Krishanti had started to build an emotional wall around himself for fear that this new family too might soon abandon him. He also struggled with fears that any closeness he might develop with his foster family could mean that they were replacing his own family and he felt he needed to resist it. He started to feel constant mistrust and tension, which came out in his worsening behaviour at school and at home. His feelings of ambivalence, coupled with a painful sense of survivor's guilt, got in the way of his being able to accept a lot of the support he was receiving in the host country.

He was anxious all the time about his family's safety, and overwhelmed with worry when he was not able to reach them by phone. At school, he struggled with memory problems, and even though he got extra support for learning a new language, he found himself often feeling confused, with his mind wandering. He was often angry and frustrated, and was easily startled and fearful at any unexpected noise.

Krishanti was referred for counselling by his social worker who was concerned that he was having trouble at school. She discussed this with him and he agreed that he might benefit from talking to someone. He arrived on time for the appointment, presenting as neatly dressed and well groomed. He and the therapist talked about what he understood about counselling and the ways they could perhaps find ways to manage his distress. The therapist emphasised that this was a safe and confidential space where he could share and explore his thoughts and feelings and identify his goals and aspirations.

Initially, he was reluctant to talk about anything other than his asylum claim, continually asking whether the therapist could help him and questioning what the point of coming here was otherwise. Speaking through an interpreter, he described in a considered and philosophical way that his father had spent all the money he had on getting him to a safe country, but he did not feel safe, and in fact felt he was about to be abandoned again. However, he also volunteered that he was 'feeling fine, happy, no problems' and it took several sessions for Krishanti and the therapist to build up enough trust in the relationship for him to share any of his more difficult feelings.

Refugee children often arrive having lost their learned trust response towards adults following the trauma of their experiences in their homeland or on the journey to safety. In all cultures, children are taught to trust and obey adults, and rely on them to keep them safe; yet exactly when they need that protection most – when they are fleeing for their lives – they are often faced with adults who betray them or hurt them physically, or abandon them with no care for their welfare. These children may even have had to learn to be wary of anyone seeming to offer them help. This usually leads to two possible responses: the inability to form bonds of trust with anyone other than the people they arrived with; or an inordinate and indiscriminate desire to please any adult. The therapist had read in Krishanti's referral form that he often missed appointments and was thought to not be engaging well with support services. However, it seemed clear to the therapist that his way of coping with his traumatic loss of family was by keeping himself distant from any new interpersonal relationships to minimise the chance of getting hurt. The therapist was therefore careful to assure him that it was up to him if he wished to come to see her, and that they would only ever talk about things he chose to bring up.

Krishanti shared that he often felt lost, and he always seemed to be fighting with himself. The therapist asked him what that meant and whether he ever felt so low he had considered harming himself. He admitted he had often had thoughts of what it would be like if he didn't exist anymore, and had sometimes considered cutting himself, although he had never done so. Exploring this further the therapist found that he had some protective factors in that he felt suicide was a sin against his religion. He also felt very strongly that his mother would never survive it if he hurt himself at all. The therapist acknowledged this, and his honesty in sharing his thoughts about such a difficult subject with her. They then talked through a risk-management plan together, detailing all the people like his social worker, doctor or foster carer he could call if he ever felt very low or afraid of hurting himself.

It is notable that separated refugee children having lost their family have had to establish relationships with professionals in creating a support network.

Back home
Mother
Father
Uncle
Auntie
Grandmother
Community
Friends

Host country
Social worker
Foster family
Teacher
Doctor
Diverse peers
Solicitor
Immigration officer

Figure 11.2: Relationships and attachments

At a cognitive level, he understood why his family had sent him away for safety reasons, yet his intense psychological yearning for his family, particularly his mother, left him confused and disempowered. He said he needed to be with his mother, that as the only son in the family he had a duty to care for his parents. The therapist pointed out to him that he appeared sad as he spoke of his mother, and he seemed close to tears and appeared to be trying hard to compose himself. He said that it would be different if he could go and see his mother and return here, but as this was not the case, he felt that he had no other choice. He reflected how he often looked at his mobile phone waiting to hear his mother's voice in vain. The therapist acknowledged the depth of the sadness he was sharing with her, to which he replied, 'It's ok, it's fine.'

He reflected that he knew the family he was living with were 'good, kind to me' but somehow he felt his 'heart is not there' and he got irritable every time they spoke to him politely.

The therapist acknowledged his courage and the determination he showed in fleeing his country and the challenging journey he made, which he initially seemed to minimise. This led to them introducing the idea of his resilience, and exploring together how that might help him in the present.

In their next meeting, using postcards which they laid out together on the floor, the therapist asked him to chose one that brought to mind a happy memory, either from his life here or in his past. He immediately chose a picture of a little boy on a donkey, and launched into a story about his brother and him going to fetch water for his mother. 'The donkey kicked my brother and he fell over, spilling his water,' he laughed, imitating his brother's surprised face until the therapist joined in the laughter as well, 'and then I laughed so much I spilled all my water too!' The therapist then pointed out that he had been able to bring his family, and his laughter, to their session, which meant they were there for him to draw on whenever he felt low. This seemed to have a positive impact and they talked about it until the end of the session. During their next sessions, they often used postcards to help him link with a more positive narrative about his family and to help him identify and express his feelings (Stedman 2003).

This allowed Krishanti and the therapist to consider his relationship with his foster family as a valuable part of his life here now, separate from his love and feelings for his own family. Over the next few weeks he reported that he was spending more time with them, and had even cooked a meal of food from his country for them. He and the therapist were also able to harness his positive memories to work on his feelings of hopelessness.

As they continued to build up their trust, Krishanti started to talk about his problems at school, particularly his anger. Using psychoeducation, he and the therapist listed what he felt when he got angry, such as feeling hot, blushing and having changes in breathing. They explored the physical reasons for this, such as increased heart rate and blood flow, and then practised some simple mindfulness breathing techniques and relaxation exercises to help him calm himself. They explored what he felt might have triggered some of his outbursts and then wrote down things to do, such as leaving the room, or slowly drinking a glass of water, to avoid this happening again. In their next session, Krishanti told the therapist that, the day before, a fellow pupil had shouted out something derogatory to him and he had simply counted to ten then quietly left the room, and for the first time since he had been here he felt in control of himself.

A significant problem faced by separated children is the loss of family or a trusted social network. With no one to bounce ideas off or to measure their feelings and responses against, separated children can start to feel that the distress and emotional difficulties they are suffering are unique to them. Krishanti had shared that he was struggling with intrusive thoughts and flashbacks and that no matter how much he tried and tried to forget the past '…it's difficult when your thoughts are like mountains'. He was unwilling to talk about this with his new friends at school, and worried they would reject him as 'crazy' because he sometimes became tearful for no apparent reason, or would jump out of his skin at any sudden noise.

Because he had never talked to anyone about this he felt sure he was the only one feeling this way, so it was important for the therapist to help him normalise his experience. Initially, after acknowledging his courage in sharing this with her, she used psychoeducation to introduce learning around the effects of extreme stress. When we experience distress and fear it is not just a mental experience but is experienced somatically, throughout our bodies. The therapist then explained a little about how our minds and bodies react to extreme danger, the so-called 'fight or flight' response when our nervous system gets us ready to take on an enemy or run for cover. She explained that the body makes certain 'stress' hormones which stimulate the blood to flow to the muscles you might need to punch or run. Your heart pounds to send blood to your limbs so that you feel very hot, and you sweat a lot to cool yourself down. Your breathing speeds up to get more oxygen to your body, and your mouth becomes dry to stop saliva getting into your stomach and starting your digestive process – a waste of precious energy. You are on edge and ready to react in a split second.

If you are able to take action to save yourself, these hormones subside and all may be well. If not, the hormones keep flooding your system. The result of this can be that even after that particular emergency has passed, your mind is still on 'red alert', primed to go at the slightest suggestion of danger, real or imaginary. And this will happen every time you are in a frightening situation after that. Bearing this in mind, the therapist encouraged Krishanti to sit quietly and notice what he was feeling in different parts of his body, where he felt tense, and how he was breathing. They then practised a mindfulness breathing technique of one long in-breath through the nose, held for three beats, followed by a full out-breath through the mouth, held for four beats. After a few minutes, he reported feeling 'very relaxed'.

The therapist suggested he should try and practise this in the morning and evening to help start to dampen down his nervous system. She also talked him through a simple grounding exercise to notice five things he could see, hear, touch, smell and taste. She explained that by concentrating on his senses like this, he would be able to divert his attention away from his inner world of panic and fear and take it to the external world of his present reality. The following week he told her he had successfully used both these techniques to help keep down a sudden sense of panic when he had been startled by the noise of a train door slamming on his journey home.

To further break down his feeling of social isolation the therapist encouraged him to consider joining a psychosocial group, where he could spend time with other children. Initially he was reluctant to commit himself because his sleep disturbances left him feeling tired all the time and with difficulty concentrating. He was also reluctant to spend time with a lot of new people. The therapist identified a local football group run by a refugee organisation and talked through the positive health and mental benefits of physical activity for dealing with stress and sleeping problems. Initially he found it hard to make the practices, often arriving up to an hour late, a pattern which was gently challenged by his coach. As his attendance improved, the coach gave him some team leadership assignments and he became more engaged, not wanting to let his team down. He started to recognise his strength as someone who could motivate his team and this gave him a purpose, along with the discipline of planning future matches. He developed trust in his coach and team mates, and became more able to allow himself to be vulnerable within an emotional relationship.

One priority in supporting a separated child is to refer them to a family tracing service in the hope that they can locate their family. This move offers the child some hope and builds a sense of trust with the outside world.

We have found that engaging separated children through creative arts and non-verbal expression in a culturally sensitive manner is an effective strategy for building a therapeutic relationship which offers them a safe path to express painful feelings and facilitates the development of the child.

Practitioners working with separated children need to be assertive in their approach and be mindful of counter-transference in the therapeutic relationship. There might be a desire to try very hard to reach an avoidant child by colluding with what they are demanding or expressing. In other cases, the child might evoke emotions that belong to the practitioner's early childhood, and at times such feelings could include a dislike of the child. Practitioners are encouraged to set up a reflective space for peer support groups or supervision where working relationships can be shared and explored to gain a better insight of the work being done.

LEARNING ACTIVITIES

Think back to your childhood.

- What was your life like when you were between 13 to 16 years of age?

- Who was around you at this time?

- Imagine if, at that age, you had travelled to a foreign country alone and you were suddenly told you could not return home: what do you think that experience would have been like for you?

■ PART 4 ■

PRACTITIONERS FIRST AID AND TOOLBOX

In Part 1 and Part 2 of this book we have focused on the issues and challenges faced by refugees in their journey to exile and how we worked with them. In Part four of this book we will be looking at the impact of these on the practitioner in order to ensure that they are able to work safely and effectively.

As part of this, because some refugees do not speak the language of the host country, it is essential to work with an interpreter which requires specific skills to manage the three-way dynamic.

Part 4 of this book is divided into three chapters:

Chapter 12 : Self-Reflective Practice and Self-Care. Working safely.

Chapter 13: Working with Interpreters. Working with an interpreter to facilitate communication with a client.

Chapter 14: Conclusion.

CHAPTER 12

SELF-REFLECTIVE PRACTICE AND SELF-CARE

After reading this chapter and completing the learning activities provided you should be able to:

- describe blind spots that need to be brought into awareness, potholes that may need to be filled in and pitfalls that would benefit from being referred to other specialist services

- focus on the benefits that come from a mindfulness attitude

- consider the risk of becoming either too caught up with or distant from refugees, due to the challenging issues they bring

- the interpersonal and intra-psychic working dynamic

- the importance of self-care to work safely.

As we described in Part 1 of this book, it is evident that the refugee phenomenon is complex and includes many traumatic events, including the loss of their homeland, separation from loved ones and challenges in the host country, which can often detrimentally impact mental health and self-identity.

While the three core principles in Part 2 are designed to foster trust, facilitate self-expression and provide useful information and skills to empower refugees in dealing with these issues, working with them can psychologically consume and often provoke powerful emotions in practitioners (Baird and Kracen 2006). Listening to traumatic narratives can also be difficult, leaving the practitioner feeling vulnerable, prone to work-related stress and experiencing feelings such as frustration, fear, contempt, envy, resentment, anger and grief (Perry, Conroy and

Ravitz 1991). In addition, limited service access in the host country and the risk of destitution can cause frustration within the client who may project anger onto the practitioner (Menzies 1959).

As the impact on the practitioner can be considerable, mindful self-reflection and supervision are essential to ensure that the practitioner is working both competently and safely and is aware of their own limitations and those of the service they provide.

Blind spots, potholes and pitfalls

We suggest there are three main areas that are important for a practitioner to be mindful of within the work they do. We refer to these areas as 'blind spots' that cannot be seen and need to be brought to light; 'potholes' that, although dangerous, can be seen and filled in; and 'pitfalls' for areas that are too dangerous to enter and definitely beyond one's competence to work in.

Refugees are people who have lost their home; by that definition this places them in a vulnerable position and in need of help. While practitioners work to ensure that their refugee clients' specific needs are met, this also places the practitioner in a position in which their own unresolved needs may be triggered which may compromise their work. For example, if the client's narrative of persecution triggers a feeling of helplessness within the practitioner that they are unable to sit with, they may do something ostensibly for the client that is primarily for the purpose of reducing their own helplessness. In a therapeutic context, this could block their client from exploring and processing their experience of persecution.

Such unresolved needs constitute what we term blind spots, outside a practitioner's awareness, which could be from an area in their childhood: for example, internal helplessness from an experience of being bullied at school, and from which, by being unable to help and protect themselves, they found validation by protecting and being helpful to others. If not processed, this childhood pattern may manifest in the practitioner's adult life and be played out through a helping profession. These unmet needs are important for practitioners to be aware of and to process in therapy. Other blind spots that the practitioner may have include their client's very different understandings of mental health symptoms, belief systems and their political ideology where the practitioner may unconsciously assume that they share the same perspective.

Potholes refer to areas that, while dangerous and potentially threatening to the work if they are not dealt with, can be filled in and made safe. In a refugee context, these include more subtle cultural differences, moderate psychological states of distress and challenging issues that can suddenly arise in the host country. For example, cultural differences in self-expression (especially when describing emotional distress), or the cultural impact of an interpreter from their community in the room, can make it difficult for a client to talk. If not factored in, these may cause the practitioner to think their client is not prepared to talk about their concerns. In reality, their client may be from a culture in which they need permission before speaking openly about their emotions, in which case they may be waiting for the practitioner to invite them to talk about their distress.

With regard to the interpreter, the client may fear that what they will say will be disclosed to their community by them, especially if they are both from a collective culture in which information tends to be disseminated throughout the entire community. In this case, it is essential that the practitioner clearly assures the client that the interpreter is bound by confidentiality and that what they disclose will be kept entirely within the room.

Psychological states of distress, we suggest, also need to be attended to carefully. If a client presents with a high level of anxiety it may be necessary for the practitioner to address this before any productive work can be done together, for example by allowing them generous time to settle, sensitively checking if they are able to engage or offering a mindful activity to ground them in the present moment.

For asylum seekers, issues that suddenly arise in the host country are often to do with the status of their asylum case. For example, if their case is refused this will need urgent intervention by a solicitor to appeal, if there are grounds for doing so. We have found it necessary sometimes to put our therapeutic work on hold to ensure that our asylum-seeking clients are able to address such issues before recommencing. As Maslow's hierarchy of needs explains, it is essential for the client's basic needs of food, shelter and belonging to be in place to create a solid foundation on which it then becomes possible to safely provide psychological intervention.

Pitfalls represent areas that are crucial to be aware of as they are beyond the remit of the organisation and require specialist agencies to address them. For example, clients who are psychologically unable to function in performing their day-to-day tasks may require a psychiatric intervention. It is imperative that practitioners proactively build working relationships with other specialist agencies to benefit their clients' wellbeing. Such an approach, by preventing clients from falling into a dangerous place (left by a service gap), will significantly reduce distress for both clients and service providers. For example, service providers may struggle to work with a torture survivor if they present with dissociative symptoms or are not coherent in their narrative. A referral to a long-term rehabilitation programme from a specialist agency may be needed to enable them to reclaim their cognitive faculties.

Having identified the clients who fit within the limitations of our service, the practitioner then needs to bring dangerous blind spots into their awareness and fill in any potholes that the work could fall into. We will illustrate how a practitioner does this by reflecting on what they are doing and why, using examples of the challenges faced when working with Priathan and Arufat. By doing so, we will show how this kept the work focused on their needs, ensuring that the service provided an effective outcome for them.

Mindfulness attitude

Williams and Kabat-Zinn (2011, p.3) explain mindfulness as a holistic approach that employs two epistemologies simultaneously: 'Western empirical science, and…the empiricism of the meditative or consciousness disciplines.' Varela and Shear (1999) explain these as providing two perspectives: a scientific view of third-person objectivity and a first-person experience of phenomenological subjective qualia (individual instances of subjective conscious experience), which each inform our work.

The phenomenological experience of our body's five senses of sight, sound, smell, taste and touch provides a resource that we always have available in order to connect with the present moment through mindfulness skills. This helps the practitioner to stay present in the face of the powerful pull of past traumatic events and future uncertainties that refugees can bring.

The third-person view provides a way of remaining objective with an attitude of compassionate curiosity and wonder. This allows the practitioner's work to be open to new scientific findings that can enhance the work through objectively observing the material that a refugee client brings and their own responses to them. This facilitates a collaborative, non-judgemental and non-pathologising way of working, which safeguards the practitioner from making assumptions about what they *think* the refugee is saying, by constantly being open to and checking their meaning with them. Checking the refugee's interpretation and the meaning of their experience is central, as issues that may be seen as 'less significant' by the practitioner may be of extreme importance to the refugee, whether this is in a positive or negative way.

For example, mental health symptoms understood from a spiritual or cultural context by a refugee may be very different to the way a mental health practitioner sees them. It is therefore important to ask what the refugee understands by their presenting symptoms from a position of not knowing, which enables an exploration of different perspectives with an open mind. This creates space for different narratives to emerge and enables the refugee to tap into their own resources to achieve a positive outcome. In this way, a mindfulness attitude allows the practitioner to see a refugee as a human being first, rather than an embodiment of the complex and challenging issues they often present with. These often literally precede them when they come to see a practitioner carrying a huge mass of paperwork relating to their multiple levels of needs.

In addition to facilitating a refugee's process, adopting a mindfulness attitude enhances the practitioner's ability to remain focused on their goals by staying connected to their own feelings, biases or assumptions. How we all see and interpret the world is impacted by different perspectives based on factors including our gender, race, religion, age, ability, culture, class, education, economics, ethnicity, sexuality and spirituality which Burnham (2011) terms Social GGRRAAACCEEESSS. For this reason, the practitioner needs to reflect on such areas of difference to find ways to remain empathic, as well as areas of similarity to ensure that they do not assume they know what their refugee client is experiencing.

To do this, the practitioner needs to be constantly aware of their thought processes and beliefs, while checking with their 'internal supervisor' as to why they respond in the way they do, which actions they take and their style of communication. It is also important for the practitioner to continually bear the refugee's needs in mind in order to check that they are always working towards meeting them. Throughout this process, the practitioner's work is also informed by the remits and limitations of the organisation and its own capacity. It is therefore essential to establish boundaries by checking the refugee's expectations and to respond to these at the onset of the working relationship so as to establish a realistic plan of how to achieve their desired outcomes.

The interpersonal and intra-psychic working dynamic

As well as working with a mindfulness attitude and establishing safe boundaries, it is important for the practitioner to be constantly aware of the risks that can beset the work. We have found that it is useful to employ the theories of Karpman's (1968) victim triangle and Freud's (1912) process of transference.

As we explored in Part 1, there is a dominant discourse that perceives refugee populations as helpless victims, which is fuelled by social media and horrific images shown on TV. This assumption of helplessness may unconsciously create an intention to help but fails to recognise refugees' strengths and positive assets, including any learned skills that they may have acquired in order to survive as a result of adversity. This assumption also creates a risk of assigning a 'victim' role of dependency to a refugee if the practitioner takes the role of rescuer. The practitioner can be at risk of disempowering the refugee by doing what they may be perfectly capable of doing for themselves, or what they may be willing to learn the necessary skills for. Consequently, the practitioner would need to be mindful to avoid taking the role of a victim with the refugee unconsciously expecting the practitioner to continue to do things on their behalf. If caught up in such a cycle it is essential for the practitioner to step back and reflect on their practice.

There may also be a parallel process of persecution between the refugee's homeland and the host country. This is because refugees have fled as a result of their country's protection structure breaking down, causing an abuse by significant others that breaches their human rights. This lack of trust in the system of authority in their country may continue on arrival in the host country due to the possibility of detention and risk of deportation. If this happens, refugees may perceive the law as an enemy to their existence. It may also impact them psychologically, causing an experience of overwhelming anxiety and fear. Consequently, they may not disclose important information about their own experience. They may also hold the view that the practitioner is an authority figure and relate to them sceptically. Even if they do see the practitioner as someone who is working for their benefit, as many refugees come from countries where the service provider is acknowledged as an expert whose solutions to the problems they present with are final, they may react to practitioners in the host country in the same way – as experts whom they are unable to challenge or question. The following example of Priathan's issues with her housing provider illustrates this.

In the therapeutic session the previous week, Priathan presented with feelings of powerlessness. She spoke softly as though her voice was fading away and the therapist struggled to hear her. She spoke of her house that was in urgent need of repairs. She reported that she had informed the accommodation provider three weeks ago, who had agreed to do the repairs but had done nothing to date. When the therapist asked her if she had reminded him, Priathan said that she was scared to 'complain' and that maybe he was busy. The therapist noticed her own feelings of irritability towards the accommodation provider and wanted to step in and help Priathan, whom the therapist perceived as being a victim. The therapist thought that it was not acceptable that Priathan was living in a house in disrepair, so she asked her if she could contact the accommodation provider on her behalf to find a resolution to this distressing issue. After the session, the therapist contacted the housing provider and expressed her client's needs in an assertive manner. The housing provider said that he would look into this matter within the next two days. On reflection, the therapist wondered whether her actions were helpful or disempowering, as she was aware from previous sessions that Priathan had past experiences of abuse and the loss of her home, which had instilled feelings of powerlessness in her. The therapist was also aware that she struggled to find her voice to articulate her needs. When the therapist checked with Priathan about why she found it difficult to remind the provider, she said that at least she had a roof over her head for her children. The therapist realised that through her soft speech and closed body language she had adapted the submissive and compliant role of a victim who lacked a voice. It was as if she was still living in the past where other people were of more importance than her.

Although Priathan had informed the housing provider about the disrepair over three weeks ago, this evoked symbolic feelings relating to the time that her husband had abandoned her and disappeared. While these feelings generated resentment, Priathan kept silent, knowing only co-operation and compliance due to her internalised early conditions of worth and being brought up as a child who had not been encouraged to voice her own needs. Priathan believed that reminding the provider about the repairs he had agreed to make would be taken as a complaint and she felt that she had no right to be complaining.

Although the therapist checked with Priathan before she acted, the therapist had unknowingly identified herself as an 'expert', which created a power imbalance that fed into her compliant and submissive attitude. The therapist's 'helpful' actions further affirmed that Priathan was not capable of making her voice heard or representing herself, hindering any effective intervention that she otherwise could have made herself, and causing her to have an experience of disempowerment.

Patel (2003) identified challenges faced by practitioners when working with people who have lost their voice through persecution and power imbalance. Checking in with your internal supervisor is important to embody a reflective attitude, always asking, 'Why am I doing what I am doing?' It is essential for the practitioner to recognise their own core beliefs, values, ethics and guiding principles and to be aware of factors that might block them from connecting to their ethical standpoint and/or professional responsibility.

In hindsight, the therapist realised that had she stayed with Priathan's feelings of helplessness they could have explored further where these feelings had come from and what purpose they served. Doing so may have created possibilities, which would have enabled Priathan to own her voice and regain the power that she had lost to her abusers. The therapist needed to look at her process in supervision and identify what she needed to learn from this. As Bughra (2004) noted, the refugee phenomena are unique to each individual, so the therapist therefore needed to understand Priathan holistically, in a way that included her coping strategies and resilience.

Clinical supervision

A maxim we employ to express the importance of supervision comes from the safety instruction before a flight that states, 'Put your own oxygen mask on first before helping others.' When up in the air this may be forgotten in the panic to help someone who is vulnerable, such as an elderly relative or child, if a problem occurs. As clients are referred to us due to their vulnerability, we risk doing the same, which is why we need to have regular supervision to remember the right course of action.

Working with Priathan at times triggered the therapist's own feelings of helplessness when her narrative resonated with her own need to look after others. On reflection, because of Priathan's complex needs, the therapist presented Priathan to her colleagues as a helpless victim, highlighting her vulnerablity. The therapist felt uncomfortable about her colleagues' feedback in supervision when, after sharing this, they questioned her feelings towards Priathan and how she had perceived her as not having the capacity to present her own needs to her housing provider. The therapist had expected recognition and affirmation of her efforts in supporting her client. Instead, supervision made her realise that she presumed what was 'best' for her client and she needed to deeply reflect on her own limitations and appreciate that she may have felt de-skilled in empowering Priathan to enhance her self-esteem in order to present her own needs. The therapist had instead felt overwhelmed listening to Priathan's painful narrative, and offered to intervene practically as a way of avoiding sitting with her own helplessness. In doing this, the therapist may have risked creating an inappropriate 'rescuer' role to make herself feel validated in her work.

In addition, as Priathan had always relied first on her mother and later on her husband to interact on her behalf, she had unconsciously transferred those feelings towards them onto her therapist. The therapist needed to be mindful not to collude with Priathan's feelings that she was projecting onto her as this would feed into Priathan's needs of dependency which continued to disempower her.

This section explains why it is essential to establish an ethical framework within which various issues – including sustaining the boundaries of the therapeutic relationship, limits of proficiency, personal issues, fears and prejudices concerning working with diversity – can be addressed in a safe and reflective manner.

Being mindful of our competence level is the place to start. Even after working for many years in which our competence is developed and assessed, there is always the risk of picking up bad habits, for example using one solution that we have generally found to be effective without thoroughly checking how this may fit with the unique dispositions of individual clients. We will now consider factors outside the practitioner's awareness, such as unconscious forces involving past relationships, which can be detrimental to the work.

The intra-psychic working dynamic

Freud's (1912) term 'transference' refers to feelings (which remain unconscious) towards a person from one's past (such as a parent) that are then inappropriately transferred onto someone else (who represents that person) in the present. If a client transfers such inappropriate feelings towards a practitioner, with whom they may also behave as if they were their parent, this could compromise their work together. Freud also observed that this process could work in the other direction – counter-transference – whereby a practitioner may experience feelings related to someone in their own past that their client's transferred feelings trigger in them. Again, if these feelings are not processed and assigned to this past relationship, it could be detrimental to the work with their client.

Supervision is a valuable space in which blind spots can be identified with the support of others. For example, the therapist working with Arufat was experiencing strong protective and angry feelings towards him. While it is natural to feel protective towards someone who has endured physical disability like Arufat, the level of concern that the therapist had towards Arufat's vulnerability seemed to go beyond this when she presented him in supervision as a completely helpless victim. The group supported her in exploring these feelings where she felt strongly protective but was also angry with the client. The supervisor asked her who the client represented in the therapist's life and what attributes they might have in common.

One of her colleagues praised the therapist's ability to work with such a complex case while stating the client was beyond the remit of the service and needed to be referred for more specialised care.

Although his response sounded supportive, the therapist was left feeling disempowered by the suggestion of referring this client elsewhere. The supervisor wondered if this was a way for practitioners to avoid challenges by offering comfort and care for each other, rather than constructive criticism that would enable the practitioners to explore their individual vulnerabilities. She also emphasised the importance of identifying compassion fatigue or burnout due to painful narratives and feelings of helplessness in being unable to meet the client's needs (Yohani 2010).

The therapist reflected how she had initially felt defensive, thinking that the supervisor had been harsh and uncaring given the impact of listening to painful narratives, now it felt comfortable to be supported and cared for by one's peers. However, the supervisor's observation was insightful and allowed the therapist to see the risk of compromising the work by being rescued. The supervisor's intervention allowed the therapist to experience her vulnerability and connect to her feelings of guilt, shame and anger. The supervisor asked again who Arufat represented in the therapist's own life and what attributes they might have in common. After some reflection, the therapist was able to connect that her feelings were coming from her relationship with her mother who had passed away three years ago. She recognised that she had unresolved feelings of guilt and shame for not being available to support her mother when she needed care. As a result, as well as wanting to care for Arufat in the way she was unable to care for her mother, the therapist also felt guilty which had been obscured by the anger she felt for not being available for her mother. This insight enabled the therapist to see her blind spot which she now held in awareness and was able to bring into her therapeutic relationship with Arufat.

This issue had created a block in the therapist's competence which resulted in her experience of being de-skilled in her work with Arufat. It was also a relief when her colleague shared similar feelings about the risks that blind spots can bring in therapeutic relationships. The colleague shared how it was beneficial to process unresolved issues in personal therapy in order to bring blind spots into awareness.

Taking Arufat's case to supervision enabled the therapist to reflect on where her feelings came from so she could process and put them in the past where they belonged. While initially the therapist mainly saw the vulnerability of Arufat, by understanding her own process she was able to work more effectively with Arufat from his frame of reference, seeing his totality which included his strengths and resilience.

This process was useful in giving the therapist the insight to see the underlying impact of Arufat's internal turmoil and conflicts as a result of his involuntary dislocation. As a political activist, he presented with feelings of guilt and shame for putting his family in danger and blamed himself for the disappearance of his daughter. This was possibly too painful for him to manage, and projecting anger onto the host country which the therapist represented was a safer way of coping with distress. Being aware that his displaced anger was not meant for the therapist but due to Arufat's own inability to process his loss and separation, allowed the therapist to be congruent with her own feelings. The therapist agreed with her supervisor that she needed to review her working contract with Arufat, how he was experiencing their working relationship and whether he found their work useful in meeting his presenting needs. The supervisor and group also discussed the remits of their service in order to manage expectations.

They also explored as a group their own anxieties and stress in their work and wondered if they were experiencing 'compassion fatigue' and secondary traumatisation from their complex casework and listening to painful narratives. Perhaps this led them to use this group space more for personal affirmation and healing?Another colleague described how he had lots of administrative work to do and had felt relieved that one of his clients had cancelled last week's session. He also reflected how he had recently turned up late for another client's appointment. This had made him feel irritated believing that he was not good enough for his clients. The group empathised with him and reaffirmed his good work. They also supported him to explore what other resources he had to help him balance his administrative and client work. Although the supervisor asked the therapist if he was working within his capacity, the therapist struggled to see options and the group wondered if the therapist was starting to show signs of exhaustion and burnout.

As a consequence, the group discussion considered the need for further training on self-care and managing boundaries. The challenges for team members to hold their own – and quite possibly the refugees' – anxieties, fears and vulnerabilities can result in stress and burnout which can reduce the ability to be present for the client and to connect to their needs. One colleague expressed the need for more support from management for frontline practitioners, and they all agreed there were areas for improvement. However, they also wondered if this could be a parallel process where they were projecting clients' distress onto management as an outlet for their interjected powerlessness, and possibly also their helplessness from their limitations on how they could make it better for the clients due to their professional position in the organisation.

In conclusion, although not all professionals are encouraged to have clinical supervision, creating a peer-reflective space in which to share and process client narratives may be beneficial in reducing the possibility of low morale and staff burnout. Yohani (2010) recognised the risk of compassion fatigue and burnout of professionals who work with a client's painful narrative and feelings of helplessness. Such a space therefore creates different perspectives where possibilities may emerge that can provide an insight on standards of service delivery and areas for improvement. It can also help a practitioner to recognise their limitations and when to seek further support or refer a case to another specialist service. This reflective space ensures safe working for both the client and the practitioner, and that safeguarding practice and expected standards are maintained.

LEARNING ACTIVITIES

Think of some relationships in your life that has triggered some strong emotions in you.

- What is it about that relationship that evokes such emotions in you?

- How might you manage these emotions to keep yourself safe

- What other time can you identify you experienced similar emotions?

- Can you see a pattern in both cases?

CHAPTER 13

WORKING WITH INTERPRETERS

A bad interpretation can lead to a miscarriage of justice, with the innocent being convicted and the guilty set free.

After reading this chapter and completing the learning activities provided, you should be able to:

- understand the importance of language in accessing local services in the host country

- understand the complexities of working in a triad where the interpreter represents two voices

- brief the interpreter before, to explain the purpose of the work, and debrief after, to clarify understanding and process any emotions

- manage dilemmas that may contain opportunities as well as challenges.

Common to many refugees is the fact that they have not only lost their homeland but also the ability to speak in a language they are familiar with if the inhabitants of the host country communicate in a different language. As specific cultural values may be woven into the fabric of the language of their country, refugees can experience this as an additional loss and feel inhibited when expressing their practical and emotional needs.

For this reason, interpreters are essential both to enable the basic human right for a refugee to have equal access to medical, psychological and social support, through a clear understanding of what they have said, and to connect to their home culture, whereby the interpreter creates a bridge to do this.

This bridge also offers the practitioner from the host country the opportunity to access their client's cultural frame of reference and, by taking this into account, communicate what their client needs to know in a manner that makes sense to them.

As the practitioner is reliant on their interpreter to facilitate this, it is essential that they organise the seating and explain their own role. This involves describing the service they are providing, any technical terms that need to be first understood to be translated, what they hope to achieve in the session, and the role that they wish the interpreter to play.

The role of the interpreter can only begin once confidentiality is agreed. It is vital that the client knows that the interpreter will not disclose anything they say in the room, which often needs to be emphasised if the interpreter is from their own community. It is also key to establish boundaries, to ensure that the interpreter stays neutral and does not give their own opinion to the client. The focus needs to be entirely on the client and what they want to say. For this purpose, the interpreter needs to appear calm and alert, with sustained eye contact, and translate all that is communicated with precision, checking anything of which they are not sure.

During the session, as the practitioner, you need to take charge and start by introducing yourself, your role and the role of your organisation. Then, ask the interpreter to introduce themselves to the client and to explain their role. If the interpreter is on the telephone and not present in the room, the practitioner needs to make it clear to the client that there is an interpreter taking part in the call and to explain what their role is. It is good practice for practitioners to use the same interpreter for follow-up sessions once the dynamic has been established and is working effectively.

Priathan reflected, 'I was disappointed when they brought a different interpreter yesterday; they said my usual interpreter was not available due to an emergency. She understands me better; the new one had facial features like my mother-in-law, as if they were related. I felt scared and submissive throughout the session and wanted it to end quickly.'

As in Priathan's case, it is common that interpreters can also represent a significant other in the client's life and this can have a positive or negative effect on the client, depending on what that other person meant to them.

If interpreters come from a refugee background with similar experiences of loss and separation, they may over identify with some of the client's narrative. In addition, the client may also represent someone they have lost. This may evoke past experiences of distress, including grief. It is important that there is an open and honest working alliance where the interpreter shares such feelings during the debriefing and the practitioner offers appropriate and empathic support to the interpreter, and is mindful of the impact that these feelings may have on their ability to interpret.

To ensure that you and your client are interpreted precisely it is important to ask the interpreter to use the first person, 'I'. This guarantees that what you say is heard by the client as coming directly from you, and that you hear your client speaking directly to you (albeit, in both cases, in the interpreter's own voice). As an extension of this, it is important for you not to have any conversations with the interpreter as this will leave your client wondering about what has been said. The other side of this is not to allow the interpreter to talk directly to the client. By following these steps both you and your client will know what is happening at all times.

In terms of the practicalities of interpreting, breaking what you need to say into digestible chunks and requesting the same of the client allows the interpreter to translate accurately. If the client becomes too upset to leave gaps, it is important to manage this sensitively and to return to what is needed whenever this becomes possible. If you notice that your interpreter is becoming upset it may help to give them a short break and also to check this after the session once the client has left. As mentioned earlier, technical terms need to be translated into language that is understandable to the client. This is particularly key in the area of mental health and especially if the client is from a culture where there may be limited terms for mental illnesses (such as depression, schizophrenia or post-traumatic stress disorder), which may instead be attributed to spiritual and magical forces (Lefley 2010). In addition, in some cultures physical and mental health are often perceived as one. Mental distress could be expressed through the body, in what is termed as somatisation. If this is the case, this requires an additional level of work to translate the client's physical presentation into psychological terminology. In this regard, observing how the client is relating in terms of mannerism, body language and physical pains while the interpreter is translating can be of great value.

When the session is completed and the client has left the room, offering the interpreter time to talk about the session allows key elements, such as the presentation of the client and any psychological impact of the material, to be unpacked.

Priathan had a session with a male key worker and a male interpreter. After the session, the service provider and the interpreter had the following debrief:

Service provider: 'I observed that you kept your arms closed throughout the session. This seemed defensive and indicated a closed body language, which may have hindered the client from sharing more openly. What do you think of this feedback?'

Interpreter: 'This is interesting feedback because I had similar thoughts and felt that your open body language was not respectful to this female client who seemed scared to look at you directly as a man. In my culture, which is also the client's culture, women do not give direct eye contact to men and I felt you came across as intimidating. My closed body language indicated humility and compassion to what she was sharing. It meant I am not bringing any of my material in the session but that I am present to listen and interpret.'

The practitioner reflected on his open body language, including his direct eye contact, as a positive way to welcome the client's material; however, he had observed the client hardly looked at him and seemed withdrawn. He was grateful the interpreter's feedback provided a valuable cultural insight, which needed to be factored in by adapting a body language that was more culturally sensitive.

As this example shows, if the interpreter is from the same culture as the client they bring great knowledge of its people, traditions and behaviour. This can help the practitioner to enhance their cultural understanding and then assess the degree to which they have fulfilled what they had hoped to do, considering (if there are more meetings scheduled) what could be incorporated in the next session to expedite this. For the interpreter, this also provides an opportunity to identify what affected them and, by expressing it, unburden some of their emotional distress.

As issues of persecution involving torture and trafficking are common in a refugee context, this distress can be considerable and it is important for the interpreter not to have to wait too long to express what has impacted them. Therefore having a debriefing session can allow the interpreter to express this and unburden some of their emotional distress.

In a therapeutic service, additional considerations are required given that sitting with and processing emotional pain is so much part of the work. It is important for the therapist to explain to the interpreter beforehand what they are seeking to do. As part of this, it is important to respect silences that occur when clients are provided with an environment in which they are able to face painful experiences that they find hard to bear, understand and articulate. It can be difficult to sit in such silences that allow the client to fully experience their pain, especially if these extend over a considerable length of time. The interpreter needs to reflect the tone used by both the client and the practitioner and include any silences or hesitations to respond. This also helps the practitioner to listen to unspoken words in the room and connect these to anxieties that the client may have.

The impulse to rescue, for example by saying something consoling, can be strong. However, as this can prevent the client from doing the work they need to do, struggling through the pain to find acceptance and, or, meaning, it is essential not to interrupt this process. From the other side, if a client is critical of the therapist or their organisation, this can be difficult for the interpreter to translate. Again, it is essential to do so, as bringing this distress into the room allows the therapist to hear and respond in a way that assures the client that their concerns and feelings are respected.

Creating a good working relationship with an interpreter is vital to the delivery of the service. This can enable any concerns raised in the session to be voiced and quickly addressed; for example, checking if the interpreter expressed everything the service provider said if their translation had taken less time, or, conversely, if they had added anything if the translation seemed to take longer.

To ensure that practitioners are working within a cultural sensitive approach, it is important that they offer interpreters space to share cultural feedback at the end of the session in order to gain an insight into the client's world, which can improve the delivery of the service.

It is also helpful to identify any concerns quickly, such as if the interpreter, whom you have observed to be generally calm, appears distressed or disengaged. This can indicate that they have been triggered by something that was said, or an issue they are sensitive to, and need to process this in the debrief.

Interpreters can face a dilemma if they meet clients in community settings outside the office, as clients may expect the interpreter to relate to them as friends based on their cultural context. While community participation is valuable, it is important that the interpreter retains their professional integrity and maintains the boundaries of their working relationship.

There are many nuances in this dynamic of working with interpreters, just as there are many different levels of competency in the interpreting field. We have found that having regular psychoeducational workshops with both practitioners and interpreters provides a good platform for sharing challenges and developing effective ways of working to enhance service delivery.

Learning Activities
Reflect on a time when you were in a place where other people around you spoke a different language.

- What was it like for you?

- How easy was it for you to communicate through an interpreter?

- What did you understand from the body language alone?

- What body had different meaning from your own?

■ CHAPTER 14 ■

CONCLUSION

We are made wise not by the recollection of our past but by the responsibility of our future.

George Bernard Shaw

We hope this book has given some insight into how the refugee-practitioner relationship can be established and then nurtured by employing a culturally sensitive therapeutic approach. For this to be effective, it is vital that the practitioner is fully cognisant of the refugee experience, understanding their frame of reference and how they see the world.

Needless to say, this is not easy. The pain refugees may have witnessed or personally experienced in their homeland – because of war, famine, disease or religious or political persecution – is scarring and leaves a lasting and profound physical and mental impact. The journey refugees then have to make to a host country can be deeply challenging and no less traumatic, and places them at the very edge of their psychological wellbeing. In fact, it's not ultimately possible for a practitioner to fully appreciate the loss and possible trauma of such people, particularly if they have not experienced this for themselves.

Yet, to be of any use, they have to try. So a little context can help. This is why, in Part 1, we offered background stories of what a refugee's life might have been like before their adversity, and then explained how their subsequent experiences may have adversely affected them. This preview prepares the practitioner at least to *empathise* with the refugee narrative.

As we have underlined in the previous pages, once established, the refugee-practitioner relationship is not straightforward – if only it were. Yet this is not much of a surprise when two people from different backgrounds come together in such troubled circumstances.

By definition, refugees are people who have lost their homes. They are individuals in desperately vulnerable positions who are in need of drastic help. Practitioners, meanwhile, have a learned expertise and a willingness to be helpful, and their role puts them in a position of feeling needed.

Yet it is these same internal needs that can at times play a negative role in a therapeutic relationship. In Part 2, therefore, we suggested a way of working that enables the practitioner to listen and empower simultaneously while being mindful of their own emotional pitfalls, in order to facilitate growth and desired outcomes (while offering their expertise, for instance, it's essential that a practitioner always works from a position of humility). In Part 4, we reminded ourselves that internal conflicts challenge the practitioner's work on various levels; and in we drew on self-care and the other direct skills needed to effectively facilitate the practitioner's work.

Take the issue of 'blind spots' that practitioners need to be aware of or sensitive to. These can include a refugee's cultural understanding towards mental health symptoms, their belief system, their spiritual belief and their political ideology. Not checking these blind spots puts the therapeutic relationship in jeopardy and can ultimately lead to a failure of service delivery. Of course, on paper, the words 'failure of service delivery' sounds horribly trivial. In practice, however, it can be devastating. In starkly human terms, it means that, for the refugee, no help is forthcoming and trauma is piled upon trauma. And that is the worst outcome of all.

This is why we are so passionate about exploring the potential complexity of the refugee-practitioner relationship and, crucially, suggesting an effective framework of ideas that may help people who have been through the refugee experience. The ideas we offer within these pages are not the only approach or even the best approach (although they work for us). They are instead an *additional* approach, which may work with some of the refugees encountered by practitioners. At the very least, we hope they evoke thought, discussion and critique that generates a more creative way of working.

Refugees are remarkable people who, after escaping trauma in their homeland, often show great strength and determination to rebuild their lives by seeking the help and support from the host country system. As practitioners ourselves, we feel privileged to work with such dynamic and resilient individuals and hence take refugees seriously as competent interpreters of their own lives. Our aim is to ensure we are working safely to stabilise and reduce distress through a psychosocial approach that offers integrated programmes of social, emotional and psychological interventions.

We recognise this is work in progress and further development will be needed to take it forwards, especially around research in evaluating this framework as an ethical approach to working with the refugee population.

FAMILY GENOGRAM

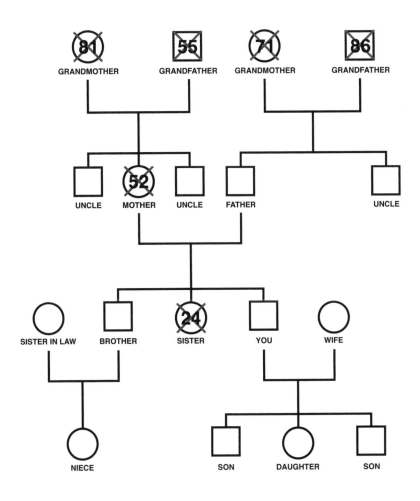

EXTERNAL FACTORS

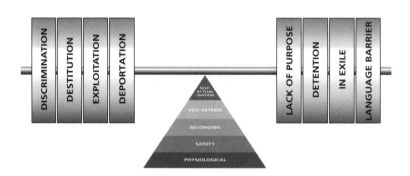

APPENDIX C

FEAR AND SADNESS

PARANOIA | LEARNED HELPLESS | HYPER VIGILANCE | FLASHBACKS

SELF-ACTUAL-ISATION
SELF-ESTEEM
BELONGING
SAFETY
PHYSIOLOGICAL

LOW SELF ESTEEM | LONELINESS | GRIEF | ALIENATION

CRISIS INTERVENTION

Anchor relationship to the present
(mindfulness skills)

Bear witness to emotional storms
(prioritising)

Bring psycho-education
(normalising)

REFERENCES

Afuape, T. (2011) *Power, Resistance and Liberation in Therapy with Survivors of Trauma.* London: Routledge.

American Psychiatric Association (2013) *Diagnostic and Statistical Manual of Mental Disorders, 5th edition.* Washington, DC: American Psychiatric Association.

Aroian, K.J. (1993) 'Mental health risks and problems encountered by illegal immigrants.' *Issues in Mental Health Nursing,* 14, 379–397.

Arredondo-Dowd, P.M. (1981) 'Personal loss and grief as a result of immigration.' *Personnel and Guidance Journal,* 59, 6, 376–378.

Baird, C. and Kracen, A.C. (2006) 'Vicarious traumatization and secondary traumatic stress: A research synthesis.' *Counselling Psychology Quarterly,* 19, 2, 181–188.

Barker, M., Vossler, A. and Langdridge, D. (eds) (2010) *Understanding Counselling and Psychotherapy.* London: Sage.

Basedow, J. and Doyle, J. (2016) *England's Forgotten Refugees: Out of the Fire and into the Frying Pan.* London: Refugee Council. Available at: www.refugeecouncil.org.uk/assets/0003/7935/England_s_Forgotten_Refugees_final.pdf accessed on 1 September 2017.

Ben-Porath, Y.S. (1991) 'The Psychosocial Adjustment.' In J. Westmeyer, C.L. Williams, and A.N. Nguyen (eds) *Mental Health Services for Refugees.* DHHS Publications No. (ADM) 91–1824. Washington, DC: US Government Printing Office.

Berry, J.W. (1997) 'Immigration, acculturation and adaptation.' *Applied Psychology: An International Review,* 46, 1, 5–68.

Bhugra, D. (2004) 'Migration and mental health.' *Acta Psychiatrica Scandinavica,* 109, 243–258.

Bion, W.R. (1959) 'Attacks on linking.' *International Journal of Psycho-Analysis,* 40, 308–315.

Bion, W.R. (1961) *Experiences in Groups and Other Papers.* London: Tavistock Publications.

Bion, W. (1962) *Learning from Experience.* London: Karnac.

Blackwell, R. (1997) 'Holding, containing and bearing witness: the problem of helpfulness in encounters with torture survivors.' *Journal of Social Work Practice: Psychotherapeutic Approaches in Health, Welfare and the Community,* 11, 2, 81–89.

Bowlby, J. (1952) *Maternal Care and Mental Health.* Geneva: World Health Organization.

Crawley, H. (2001) *Refugees and Gender: Law and Process.* London: Jordan Publishing Limited.

Dearden, L. (2016) 'Record number of refugees would make 21st biggest country in the world with population bigger than the UK.' *Independent,* 14 September, 2016. Available at: www.independent.co.uk/news/world/politics/refugee-crisis-asylum-seekers-migrants-numbers-country-21st-largest-syria-iraq-europe-afghanistan-a7307196.html accessed on 29 October 2017.

Dennis, J. (2012) *Not a Minor Offence: Unaccompanied Children Locked Up as Part of the Asylum System.* London: Refugee Council. Available at: www.refugeecouncil.org.uk/assets/0002/5945/Not_a_minor_offence_2012.pdf accessed on 1 September 2017.

Easteal, P.W. (1996) 'Violence against immigrant women in the home.' *Alternative Law Journal,* 21, 2, 53–57.

Eastmond, M. (1989) *The Dilemmas of Exile: Chilean Refugees in the United States.* Unpublished doctoral thesis, Department of Social Anthropology, Gothenburg University, Sweden.

Eisenbruch, M. (1990) 'Cultural Bereavement and Homesickness.' In S. Fisher and C.L. Cooper (eds) *On the Move: The Psychology of Change and Transition.* Chichester: Wiley.

Eisenbruch, M. (1991) 'From posttraumatic stress disorder to cultural bereavement: diagnosis of Southeast Asian refugees.' *Social Science and Medicine,* 33, 673–680.

Engel, G.L. (1977) 'The need for a new medical model: a challenge for biomedicine.' *Science,* 196, 129–36.

Erikson, E.H. (1968) *Identity:Youth and Crisis.* New York: W.W. Norton.

Farbey, J. (2002) 'The Refugee Condition. Legal and Therapeutic Dimensions.' In K. Renos Papadopoulos (ed.) *Therapeutic Care for Refugees: No Place Like Home.* The Tavistock Clinic Series. New York: Karnac.

Felder, J.N., Dimidjian, S. and Segal, Z. (2012) 'Collaboration in mindfulness-based cognitive therapy.' *Journal of Clinical Psychology,* 68, 2, 179–186.

Freud, S. (1894) 'Studies on Hysteria Chapter III Theoretical Section: Unconscious ideas and ideas inadmissible to consciousness - Splitting of the mind. SE.' *The Standard Edition of the Complete Psychological Works of Sigmund Freud,* 2, 222-239.

Freud, S. (1912) 'The Dynamics of Transference.' In J. Strachey (ed.) (1978) *The Standard Edition of the Complete Psychological Works of Sigmund Freud, Volume XII.* London: Hogarth Press.

Garcia-Peltoniemi, R.E. (1991) 'Clinical Manifestations of Psychopathology.' In J. Westmeyer, C.L. Williams and A.N. Nguyen (eds) *Mental Health Services for Refugees.* DHHS Publications No. (ADM) 91–1824. Washington, DC: US Government Printing Office.

Hanson, E. and Vogel, G. (2012) 'The Impact of War on Civilians.' In L. Lopez Levers (ed.) *Trauma Counseling: Theories and Interventions.* New York: Springer Publishing Company.

Hathaway, J. (1991) *The Law of Refugee Status.* Toronto: Butterworths.

Harris, J. R. (1998) *The Nurture Assumption: Why Children Turn out the Way They Do.* New York: The Free Press.

Henningsen, P., Zimmermann, T., Sattel, H. (2003) 'Medically unexplained physical symptoms, anxiety, and depression: a meta-analytic review.' *Psychosom Med.,* 65, 528–533.

Herman, J.L. (1992) *Trauma and Recovery: The Aftermath of Violence.* New York: Basic Books.

Kabat-Zinn, J. (1994) *Wherever You Go, There You Are: Mindfulness Meditation for Everyday Life.* London: Piatkus.

Karpman, S. (1968) 'Fairy tales and script drama analysis.' *Transactional Analysis Bulletin,* 7, 26, 39–43.

Kinyon, J. and Lasater, I. (2015) *Choosing Peace: New Ways to Communicate to Reduce Stress, Create Connection, and Resolve Conflict (Mediate Your Life: A Guide to Removing Barriers to Communication) (Volume 1).* Park City UT: Mediate Your Life.

Kunz, E. F. (1973) 'The refugee in flight: kinetic models and forms of displacement.' *International Migration Review,* 7, 125–146.

Lefley, H.P. (2010) 'Mental Health System in a Cross-Cultural Context.' In T.L. Scheid and T.N. Brown (eds) *A Handbook for the Study of Mental Health: Social Contexts, Theories and Systems* (pp.135–161). New York: Cambridge University Press.

Madsen, W.C. (1999) *Collaborative Therapy with Multi-Stressed Families: From old problems to new futures.* New York, NY: Guilford Press.

Madsen, W. C. (2007) *Collaborative therapy with multi-stressed families,* Second Edition. New York, NY: The Guilford Press.

Martín-Baró (1964) 'La terapia no directiva de Carl Rogers' ['The non-directive therapy of Carl Rogers']. *Antena,* 8, 15–24.

Maslow, A.H. (1943) 'A theory of human motivation.' *Psychological Review,* 50, 370–96. Available at: www.oed.com accessed on 1 September 2017.

Melzak, S. (2009). 'Psychotherapeutic Work with Children and Adolescents Seeking Refuge from Political Violence.' In M. Lanyado and A. Horne (eds) *The Handbook of Child and Adolescent Psychotherapy: Psychoanalytic Approaches,* 2nd edition. Hove: Routledge.

McGoldrick, M., and Gerson, R. (1985). *Genograms in family assessment.* New York: W. W.Norton & Co.

McIntyre, P. (2012) *Between a Rock and a Hard Place: The Dilemma Facing Refused Asylum Seekers.* London: Refugee Council. Available at: www.refugeecouncil.org.uk/assets/0000/1368/Refugee_ Council_Between_a_Rock_and_a_Hard_Place_10.12.12.pdf accessed on 1 September 2017.

Melucci, A. (1996) *Challenging Codes: Collective Action in the Information Age.* Cambridge: Cambridge University Press.

Memmi, A. (1957) *The Colonizer and the Colonized.* Boston: The Orion Press.

Menzies-Lyth, I. (1989) *The Dynamics of the Social: Selected Essays, Volume 2.* London: Free Association Books.

Moss, W.J., Ramakrishnan, M., Storms, D., Henderson, *et al.* (2006) 'Child health in complex emergencies.' *Bulletin of the World Health Organization,* 84, 1, 58–64.

Myerhoff, B. (1986) 'Life Not Death in Venice: Its Second Life.' In V.W. Turner and E.M. Bruner (eds) *The Anthropology of Experience.* Chicago, IL: University of Illinois Press.

NHS Choices (2017) *Why people attempt suicide.* Available at: www.nhs.uk/Conditions/Suicide/ Pages/Causes.aspx accessed on 20 August 2017.

Padilla, A.M. and Perez, W. (2003) 'Acculturation, social identity, and social cognition: a new perspective.' *Hispanic Journal of Behavioral Sciences* 25, 1, 35–55.

Papadopoulos, R.K. (2001) 'Refugees, therapists and trauma: systemic reflections.' *Context: The Magazine of the Association for Family Therapy,* 54, 5–8.

Papadopoulos, R. (ed.) (2002) *Therapeutic Care for Refugees: No Place Like Home.* London: Karnac Books.

Papadopoulos, R. K. (2004). 'Trauma in a systemic perspective: theoretical, organizational and clinical dimensions.' Paper presented at the 14th Congress of the International Family Therapy Association, Istanbul.

Papadopoulos, R.K. (2007). 'Refugees, trauma and adversity activated development.' *European Journal of Psychotherapy and Counselling,* 9, 3, 301–312.

Papadopoulos, R. K. (2011) 'A psychosocial framework in working with refugees.' Published originally in Korean in *Nancen,* 16 December, 2011. Available at: http://nancen.tistory.com/696 accessed on 31 October 2017.

Patel, N. (2003) 'Speaking with the Silent: Addressing Issues of Disempowerment When Working with Refugee People.' In R. Tribe and H. Raval (eds) *Working with Interpreters in Mental Health.* New York: Brunner Routledge.

Pearce, W.B. (1994) *Interpersonal Communication: Making Social Worlds.* New York: HarperCollins.

Perry, B.D, Conroy, L and Ravitz, A. (1991). Persisting psychophysiological effects of traumatic stress: The memory of "states". *Violence Update 1,* 8, 1–11. Accessed at www.childtrauma.org/ctamaterials/memory_states.asp.

Phillimore, J. (2011) 'Refugees, acculturation strategies, stress and integration.' *Journal of Social Policy,* 40, 3 575–593.

Pope, K. and Garcia-Peltoniemi, R. (1991) 'Responding to victims of torture: clinical issues, professional responsibilities, and useful resources.' *Professional Psychology: Research and Practice,* 22, 269-276.

Refugee Council (2017) *Who's who.* Available at: www.refugeecouncil.org.uk/policy_research/the_truth_about_asylum/the_facts_about_asylum accessed on 30 October 2017.

Rogers, C. (1957) 'The necessary and sufficient conditions of therapeutic personality change.' *Journal of Counseling Psychology,* 21, 95–103.

Rogers, C.R. (1959) 'A Theory of Therapy, Personality and Interpersonal Relationships as Developed in the Client-centered Framework.' In Koch, S. (Ed.), *Psychology: A Study of a Science. Volume 3. Formulations of the Person and the Social Context.* New York.

Stedman, R. C. (2003) 'Is it really just a social construction?: the contribution of the physical environment to sense of place.' *Society & Natural Resources,* 16, 8, 671–685. Available at: www.researchgate.net/publication/233245425_Is_It_Really_Just_a_Social_Construction_The_Contribution_of_the_Physical_Environment_to_Sense_of_Place accessed on 23 September 2017.

Tribe, R. (2002) 'Mental health of refugees and asylum seekers.' *Advances in Psychiatric Treatment* 8, 240–248.

UN General Assembly (1951) 'Convention Relating to the Status of Refugees, 28 July 1951.' In *United Nations, Treaty Series, Volume 189.* Available at: www.refworld.org/docid/3be01b964.html accessed on 21 September 2017.

Unicef (2016) *Danger Every Step of the Way. A Harrowing Journey to Europe for Refugee and Migrant Children.* Available at: www.unicef.org/emergencies/childrenonthemove/files/Child_Alert_Final_PDF.pdf accessed on 1 September 2017.

Universal Declaration of Human Rights 1948. Available at: www.amnesty.org.au/how-it-works/what-are-human-rights accessed on 1 September 2017.

Van der Veer, G. (1992) *Counselling and Therapy with Refugees.* Chichester: Wiley.

Varela, F. J. and Shear, J. (1999) 'First-person methodologies: why, when and how?' *Journal of Consciousness Studies,* 6, 2–3, 1–14.

Westermeyer, J. (1991) 'Models of Mental Health Services.' In J. Westmeyer, C.L. Williams, and A.N. Nguyen (eds) *Mental Health Services for Refugees,* DHHS Publications No. (ADM) 91–1824. Washington, DC: US Government Printing Office.

White, M. and Epston, D. (1990) *Narrative Means to Therapeutic Ends.* New York: Norton.

Williams, J. M. G. and Kabat-Zinn, J. (2011) 'Mindfulness: diverse perspectives on its meaning, origins, and applications.' *Contemporary Buddhism,* 12, 1, 1–18.

Winnicott, D.W. (1953) 'Transitional objects and transitional phenomena – a study of the first not-me possession.' *International Psycho-Analysis,* 34, 89–97.

Winnicott, D.W. (1971) *Playing and Reality.* London: Routledge.

Yohani, S. (2010) 'Nurturing hope in refugee children during early years of postwar adjustment.' *Children and Youth Services Review,* 32, 865–873.

INDEX

ABOUT THE AUTHORS

Angelina Jalonen is a BACP registered psychological therapist and therapeutic supervisor, with masters in Refugee Care from the University of Essex, Angelina has over 17 years' experience of working directly with asylum seekers and refugees in meeting their psychosocial needs. As a Therapeutic Services Manager, Angelina is responsible for designing and implementing therapeutic programmes at the Refugee Council both in London and at the regional offices. She has also been a foster parent to unaccompanied asylum seeking children for 7 years where she worked closely with social services and educational sectors. Angelina provides capacity building training and lectures at universities on 'Psychosocial perspectives to mental distress in refugee population'. As well as her work with refugees, Angelina has created an empowering practice called Sunshine Building Bridges in Kenya which offers education and vocational skills to the less privileged members of the society.

Paul Cilia La Corte is a BACP registered Senior Psychological Therapist. With a master's degree in Refugee Care from the University of Essex, Paul has been providing one-to-one counselling to refugees and asylum seekers for over seven years and leads on the development of the Therapeutic Care Framework. This framework emphasises a psychosocial perspective that responds to the multiple and complex needs with which refugees and asylum seekers present. Paul also delivers talks and training on 'Improving mental health for asylum seekers and refugees'.